RAND | NATIONAL DEFENSE RESEARCH INSTITUTE

Options for Department of Defense Total Workforce Supply and Demand Analysis

Potential Approaches and Available Data Sources

Shanthi Nataraj, Christopher Guo, Philip Hall-Partyka, Susan M. Gates, Douglas Yeung

Prepared for the Office of the Secretary of Defense

For more information on this publication, visit www.rand.org/t/rr543

Library of Congress Control Number: 2014952046
ISBN: 978-0-8330-8597-9

Published by the RAND Corporation, Santa Monica, Calif.

© Copyright 2014 RAND Corporation

RAND® is a registered trademark.

Support RAND
Make a tax-deductible charitable contribution at
www.rand.org/giving/contribute

www.rand.org

Preface

Under 10 U.S.C. 115b (National Defense Authorization Act [NDAA] Fiscal Year [FY] 2010, Section 1108), the Office of the Under Secretary of Defense for Personnel and Readiness (OUSD [P&R]) has responsibility for developing and implementing the strategic workforce plan for the U.S. Department of Defense (DoD).

This research report provides an overview of the approaches used for the purposes of workforce analysis and of the data sources that DoD could use to inform such analyses. This overview will be useful to workforce managers at DoD and elsewhere as they assess which approaches will best meet their needs and how existing data sources might need to be improved in order to support such analyses.

This research was sponsored by the Deputy Assistant Secretary of Defense for Civilian Personnel Policy (DASD [CPP]) and conducted within the Forces and Resources Policy Center of the RAND National Defense Research Institute, a federally funded research and development center sponsored by the Office of the Secretary of Defense, the Joint Staff, the Unified Combatant Commands, the Navy, the Marine Corps, the defense agencies, and the defense Intelligence Community.

For more information on the RAND Forces and Resources Policy Center, see http://www.rand.org/nsrd/ndri/centers/frp.html or contact the director (contact information is provided on the web page).

Contents

Figures, Tables, and Boxes

Summary

Under 10 U.S.C. 115b (National Defense Authorization Act Fiscal Year 2010, Section 1108), the Office of the Under Secretary of Defense for Personnel and Readiness has responsibility for developing and implementing the U.S. Department of Defense's (DoD's) strategic workforce plan, in consultation with the Office of the Under Secretary of Defense for Acquisition, Technology, and Logistics. In keeping with the legislative requirements, DoD seeks to accelerate improvements to the department's workforce data, forecasting methods, tools, and analysis to develop a comprehensive, measurable planning process that drives strategic human capital management decisions within the Total Force construct. To achieve this aim, DoD needs to improve upon the tools available to analyze the civilian workforce DoD-wide and develop the data resources and capacity to engage in total workforce analysis.

Workforce planning can be defined as having the "right number of people with the right set of skills and competencies in the right job at the right time" (Vernez et al., 2007). The basic goal is to close any gaps between the human resources an organization needs to carry out its mission (demand) and the human resources it has (supply). Effective workforce planning not only aids organizations in using resources effectively and ensuring that the organization has the staff needed to accomplish its objectives; it also can help organizations identify and mitigate workforce risks.

The workforce planning process may be divided into five major steps (adapted from Office of Personnel Management [OPM] guidance [OPM, "OPM's Workforce Planning Model," undated]) and summarized in Figure S.1:

1. **Set strategic direction.** Identify the ways in which the organization's long-term and short-term goals might affect workforce planning. This is often accomplished through an *environmental scan*, in which an organization identifies internal drivers (such as changes in the organization's mission) and external drivers (such as economic conditions) that may affect the organization's human resource needs and gathers high-level information about these drivers.

2a. **Determine workforce supply.** Determine what the current workforce looks like and how it is likely to evolve over time, based on current trends, existing personnel policies and practices, and drivers identified in Step 1. Workforce supply projection usually begins with analyzing human resources data to

Figure S.1
Overview of the Workforce Planning Process

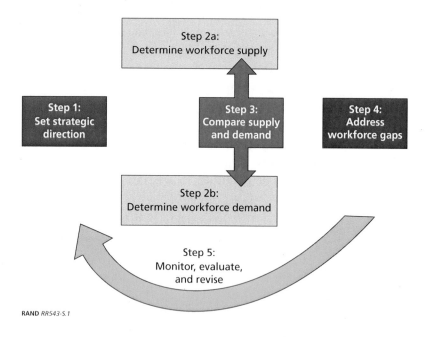

RAND RR543-S.1

understand the historical patterns of worker separation, hiring, transfers, promotions, and other key activities. Historical patterns are then projected into the future, using one of a variety of techniques, to arrive at future workforce supply projections. Projections may take into account anticipated changes in worker behavior, human resource policies, or other conditions that are likely to make future patterns deviate from historical patterns.

2b. **Determine workforce demand.** Use information about current and projected future workload, as well as drivers identified in Step 1, to project what future workforce requirements will be. Workforce demand projection can take multiple forms, but typically involves three stages: (1) Assess current workload and workforce productivity, (2) project workload into the future, and (3) project future productivity and apply to future workload in order to derive future workforce size.

3. **Compare the demand with the supply.** Identify gaps between supply (the projected future workforce from Step 2a) and demand (the desired future workforce from Step 2b). Gaps are not limited strictly to a difference between the sizes of workforce supply and demand; they can also be inferred from assessments of organizational effectiveness and assessments of workforce stress. A supply/demand gap can be manifested in terms of low effectiveness or high stress.

4. **Develop and implement an action plan.** Identify and implement strategies to close gaps between supply and demand that were identified in Step 3.

5. **Monitor, evaluate, and revise.** Monitor progress toward the goals established in the action plan, and revise strategies as needed.

Prior research suggests that workforce planning in DoD is more complicated than this simple framework would suggest because the activities can occur at different levels of the organization (Gates et al., 2006). Analyses conducted at different organizational levels in support of workforce planning serve different purposes. Managers may need to access different data and employ different analytical approaches, depending on their objectives.

This report reviews the approaches used in the private sector and in government organizations for tackling Steps 2a and 2b of the workforce analysis process described above—namely, determining workforce supply and demand—and assesses the availability of data needed to apply such approaches to DoD total workforce analysis.

Choices in Workforce Planning and Analysis

When approaching workforce analysis, managers are faced with critical choices about the scope of analysis, the level of aggregation, the type of projection techniques that will be used, the time period over which projections will be made, and the data sources to be used. These choices apply to both demand and supply analysis. The key considerations for each choice area are summarized in Table S.1.

Although supply and demand analysis are often considered in isolation of one another, it is important for managers to recognize that historical stocks and flows of workers represent *equilibrium* outcomes—a combination of both supply and demand factors. Historical separation rates reflect the willingness of current workers to continue working (supply), which is in turn influenced by a variety of factors that are internal to the organization (for example, how current management is viewed by employees), as well as external factors (for example, the unemployment rate). Separation rates may also reflect early retirement incentive packages offered by the company because of reduced staffing needs (demand).

Workforce Supply Analysis

Supply analysis can involve an examination of past, present, or future workforce supply. Workforce supply projections are almost always based on projecting historical workforce patterns into the future. This may be a reasonable assumption when an organization is experiencing

Table S.1
Key Considerations for Workforce Planners

Choice Area	Key Considerations
Scope	• How much of the workforce to analyze • Whether to analyze subpopulations and, if so, which ones • Whether to analyze only the number of workers or other characteristics as well • Whether to consider workers outside the organization
Level of aggregation	• How large and heterogeneous the workforce is • Whether it is possible to generalize across workers within a level of aggregation • How many workers there are at a given level • At what level questions need to be answered to address strategic questions • Cost associated with conducting workforce analysis at a particular level
Type of projection technique	Quantitative • Deterministic models vs. stochastic models • Descriptive models vs. optimization models • Analytic techniques vs. simulation techniques • Aggregate models vs. agent-based models Qualitative • Number of scenarios • Method for gathering information
Time period for forecasting	• Longer time periods are used for organization-wide strategic planning; shorter time periods are used for tactical planning at the business unit level

a relatively stable period but is unlikely to be true during times of major change.

Historical trends can be useful in providing a baseline forecast. However, managers should always use their judgment to assess whether historical trends are likely to continue in the future and incorporate those insights into their planning. We review several categories of supply analysis tools in this report. Many of the tools allow the user to change historical rates to reflect projected changes in both supply factors (for example, reduced availability of certain types of workers) and demand factors (for example, a hiring freeze).

Stock-and-Flow Models

The most common type of workforce supply model—the stock-and-flow model—begins with a stock of workers in a particular year and uses estimates of worker flows to project the stock in subsequent years. Two important variants of stock-and-flow models are "push" models and "pull" models. "Push" models move workers through the system based on the historical probability (or some other probability) of transitioning from one state to another. They take these transition probabilities as given and estimate what the future supply will be based on those flows. This variant is used when transitions are not dependent on the availability of positions. "Pull" models move workers based on whether positions are available. Pull models take workforce demand as given, and the models are used to estimate hiring and promotion rates needed to fill positions.

Stock-and-flow models are easy to use and easy to understand. Although individual projections are deterministic and strongly driven by assumptions, users who are adept at manipulating these models can explore a wide range of assumptions (scenarios) and gain insight into the range of possible outcomes. However, stock-and-flow models cannot be used to identify the optimal workforce needed to achieve a particular objective.

Systems Dynamics Models

Systems dynamics models are similar to stock-and-flow models but incorporate feedback loops and allow potential time delays between inputs and output. The key feature that differentiates this type of model from a standard stock-and-flow model is that it is a *closed loop* system. For instance, new hiring affects the number of junior employees, which affects the number of senior employees, which in turn affects recruiting (new hiring) decisions.

A key advantage of a systems dynamics model is that it can explicitly model the ways in which changes in one part of the system can affect other parts of the system; a change in the availability of vacant positions, for example, affects promotion opportunities, and thus affects retention rates. However, this feature also makes a systems dynamics model more difficult to develop and less transparent to users than a standard stock-and-flow model. In addition, systems dynamics models must typically be solved by computer simulation rather than analytically, so the availability of computing resources and the time required to solve the model will factor into whether a systems dynamics model is appropriate for a particular application.

Regression Models

Regression methods explicitly recognize that there are random elements that affect outcomes of interest and introduce "disturbances" to account for such elements. Time-series methods may forecast the future value of an outcome of interest based on past values of that outcome, as well as on past values of random disturbances. Cross-sectional methods model an outcome of interest as a function of other variables observed at the same time, as well as a random disturbance term. Panel data methods combine both time-series and cross-sectional approaches.

There are few examples of purely regression-based workforce supply models. More commonly, regression methods are used to improve forecasts of transition rates that are then used in other models. For example, while simple stock-and-flow models assume that transition rates are equal to average historical rates, time-series methods may be used to extrapolate historical rates into the future. In addition, cross-sectional methods may be used to relate workforce characteristics to separation rates, so that projected separation rates may be adjusted to accommodate anticipated changes in workforce composition.

A key advantage of regression models is that they explicitly account for uncertainty associated with the outcomes of interest and generate a range of future estimates. They can also be used for projecting historical trends into the future and for estimating the effects of changing workforce characteristics on supply. However, the results of these models may change substantially when different modeling choices are used. Also, regression models cannot be used to identify the optimal workforce needed to achieve a particular objective.

Optimization Models

Whereas stock-and-flow, systems dynamics, and regression models are predictive in nature because they project future labor supply based on historical trends, optimization models are goal-oriented. These models identify policies that optimize certain metrics given a set of constraints, such as future manpower requirements. These models are useful for a workforce planner who knows how many personnel he or she wants in the future but is unsure of how he or she should hire and promote to meet that objective. They can also be useful for a workforce planner who wants to meet a specific and quantifiable goal, such as minimizing cost.

The goals that the planner seeks to achieve and the requirements the planner faces are modeled with *objective functions* and *constraints,* respectively. Optimization models find solutions that maximize or minimize the objective functions subject to the user-specified constraints. The objective functions and constraints together form the mathematical program, a mathematical expression of the problem facing a workforce planner. A mathematical program may have only one objective function—for example, minimize cost—or may have multiple objective functions—for example, minimize cost and maximize readiness. Setting up a mathematical program requires selecting and parameterizing mathematical expressions capturing objective functions and constraints. It is often not a trivial task to even decide what is an objective and what is a constraint. For example, a workforce planner may wish to minimize cost subject to a few known constraints on readiness or may wish to minimize cost and maximize some metric related to readiness. The two approaches will yield different mathematical programs to solve within an optimization model.

Optimization models are not frequently used for manpower planning. Few manpower planners have training in optimization techniques, and established mathematical programs for workforce planning do not exist.

Simulation Techniques

Whereas simple models can be solved analytically, more complex models may not have an analytic solution; in this case, the relationships that constitute the model may be simulated using a computer. Although simulation models are often classed as a separate type of model, simulation techniques can be applied to many types of workforce models. For example, systems dynamics models, described earlier, are often solved using simulation techniques.

For workforce analysis purposes, analysts may seek to model complex individual worker behavior. For example, RAND has developed a dynamic retention model that analyzes the stay-leave decisions made by individual military members; this model assumes that individuals maximize their utility and compares future income streams from military versus civilian positions. Stochastic elements are incorporated by assuming random shocks in each year. After estimating the parameters of the model, the model simulates the behavior of individuals under alternative policy regimes (Mattock, Hosek, and Asch, 2012) and then aggregates the individual results to estimate the overall effect of the policy regime.

Simulation techniques may also be more appropriate than analytic techniques for modeling small employee populations, since they can be developed to capture decisionmaking by individual employees. However, the application of complex, agent-based simulation models to large populations of employees may require more computational power and time or may need more detailed data than an organization has available.

Replacement Charts and Succession Planning

Replacement charts involve identifying potential vacancies in higher-level positions, as well as how those vacancies could be filled by lower-level employees. Unlike the methods described above, replacement charts and succession planning identify specific individuals who are currently in the organization and who could be promoted. The exercise also helps to highlight internal competency gaps, which could be addressed through training or external hiring. These tools would typically be used to ensure smooth transitions for senior-level positions, rather than for overall workforce planning.

Workforce Demand Analysis

Determining workforce demand involves identifying the total number of workers, the type of workers (military, civilian, or contractor), and the job competencies needed to maintain an organization's missions and goals. Demand often can be more difficult to forecast than supply because of the sheer number of environmental and organizational factors that influence demand. Consequently, a number of quantitative and qualitative techniques are available to forecast workforce demand, and, in practice, the decision of which technique to employ will depend on the size, expertise, and resources available to the organization.

Regardless of the technique, there are three basic steps in projecting future workforce demand. First, an organization will assess current workforce demand and productivity, usually by relating workload to the required workforce. The second step is to project workload into the future. The third step is to project worker productivity (estimated in Step 1) into the future and apply it to the future workload (from Step 2) in order to ultimately project the required future workforce size. Most projection approaches involve some sort of assumption (implicit or explicit) about the correct level of productivity to be applied into the future and do so with varying degrees of sophistication and access to historical data. Workforce demand projections are derived through quantitative or qualitative techniques.

Quantitative Techniques for Projecting Workforce Demand

Both the most simplistic and the most accessible technique, ratio analysis estimates future demand based on ratios between assumed demand drivers (number of items manufactured, number of clients served) and the total number of workers required. These ratios are based on current data and do not require significant historical data collection (Bulmash, Chhinzer, and Speers, 2010).

Time-series analysis builds upon the reasoning of ratio analysis by tracking a ratio over a number of time periods in order to incorporate historical trends and changes in productivity. This technique assumes that *historical* workload and *historical* productivity are indicative of future workload and productivity. Time-series analysis is easy to implement. However, it is limited to tracking only one ratio or performance index over time.

Regression analysis is based on the statistical relationship between *multiple* productivity ratios and demand drivers tracked over time and the number of workers demanded. Regression analysis assumes that the relationship between demand drivers, productivity ratios, and workforce will remain stable over time. Regression models are particularly well-suited to mature organizations with relatively stable workforces and external environments. However, they do require detailed historical data on multiple variables, and new models need to be developed for different subpopulations. When using regression analysis, managers are cautioned not to assume that current relationships between workload and workforce are optimal, especially in situations when organizations undergo rapid change.

Benchmarking analysis is an approach in which a certain gold standard number of workers needed to execute a certain workload is identified and then extrapolated to a new population. This is a different way of identifying a productivity ratio; whereas the other examples are based on current/historical patterns, this is based on *exemplars*. This approach assumes that the benchmark standard represents an optimal requirement. Challenges of benchmarking arise in identifying the proper benchmark and in extrapolating it to a different population.

Input-output models translate activities of an organization into workforce demand requirements. The first step is to split the total amount of value that an organization produces into values from various categories of activities. Simple rules are used to characterize relationships between these categories—generally these relationships are assumed to be linear. The value of each activity category is used as a proxy for the cost of labor in producing that activity. These rules are then applied together to determine how external demands on an organization's activities affect the number of workers required to perform these activities. This technique has been used by the Total Army Analysis and the Generating Force-to-Operator model (Camm et al., 2011; Nataraj et al., 2014).

Qualitative Techniques for Projecting Workforce Demand

A common workforce demand projection technique is to use direct managerial judgment (Ward, 1996). Organizations aggregate the forecasts of individual managers regarding the demand for employees in the skill groups or job families in their area. These forecasts include not only current head count requirements, but also a best-guess estimate of how these head counts may change because of anticipated changes in productivity or demand drivers. This approach provides managers with flexibility in identifying and prioritizing the workforce. However, some managers may be better than others at forecasting workforce requirements, and managers may focus on different workforce characteristics, making it difficult to aggregate responses. For this reason, many organizations impose some structure on the development of workforce demand projections.

The best-known structured qualitative technique for projecting future demand is the Delphi method, which was developed by RAND as a more formalized approach to eliciting and integrating expert opinion (Dalkey and Helmer-Hirschberg, 1962). It follows an iterative process where experts provide feedback on each other's views with the goal of eventually leading to a dependable consensus of opinion. Although forecasts generated through these methods may be criticized as subjective, they tend to be well-received within the organization and often outperform quantitative techniques.

The Delphi method is particularly useful for situations with limited or uncertain historical data, changing government policy, specific educational patterns, new technology leading to evolving skill levels, and dynamic changes in work processes, which would affect worker productivity (Gatewood and Gatewood, 1983).

The nominal group technique process is a related approach that differs from Delphi in that it allows for face-to-face interaction among a panel of experts (generally managers) to discuss an organizational issue.

Unlike most other qualitative techniques that result in a single demand scenario, scenario analysis produces multiple estimates of workforce demand. Each estimate is contingent on a different set of assumptions about the organization's economic outlook. A range of scenarios is generated through face-to-face expert brainstorming sessions, and the interactive nature of expert discussion encourages innovative thinking and consideration of the future that might be missed in other approaches. This technique recognizes the high level of uncertainty about the future and the large number of factors that can affect demand. Scenario analysis is particularly good for dynamic organizations experiencing large changes, where the past is not the best predictor of the future. While scenario analysis is able to explore the entire range of possible scenarios, this method is not designed to assign probabilities to each scenario, and therefore is less effective at providing a single expected value for workforce demand.

Combining Qualitative and Quantitative Approaches in Projecting Workforce Demand

Quantitative methods suffer primarily from the lack of systematic data collection. Identifying correct demand drivers and measures of productivity, which are relevant currently and in the future, requires careful forethought and organization. Collecting historical data on these factors takes time, and a small sample size will affect model accuracy. Qualitative methods are often costly to implement and suffer from validity issues because of their subjective nature. As a result, many organizations apply a combination of quantitative and qualitative techniques—in either a top-down or a bottom-up way.

A top-down approach begins with historical data of total staffing levels and uses regression analysis to derive a relationship between the number of workers required and measures of the workload. However, both quantitative and qualitative demand drivers can be considered in a combined approach. For example, the Sustainment and Acquisition Composite Model is a top-down approach that employs both quantitative and qualitative techniques to estimate the workforce size requirements for weapon system acquisition program offices.

A bottom-up approach begins with detailed estimates of the labor required for each piece of work and then aggregates the estimates to calculate the total staffing level required. An example of this approach is the Army Material Systems Analysis Activity Acquisition Center Standard.

In general, top-down models require less data than bottom-up models and are easier to construct. Historical staffing data, including measures of skill level and experience, are readily available. In contrast, special data collection is often needed to support bottom-up approaches. However, just as with traditional regression analysis, the top-down approach assumes that historical staffing-to-workload ratios are appropriate and will hold in the future. Bottom-up models are less tied to that assumption.

Data Availability

DoD has rich data on workforce supply, which is reflected in personnel data systems. These systems provide information on the "faces"—the people who are doing the work. It also has detailed data on workforce demand or requirements, which are contained in manpower databases. We reviewed existing data sources in order to assess their ability to support workforce analysis at the functional community or occupation level from a total force perspective.

We identified three key limitations of the data that impede this aim.

In most cases, personnel and manpower data are maintained separately, and individual "faces" in the personnel data are not linked with specific "spaces" in the manpower data, thus creating a challenge for identifying positions that remain unfilled. Although some data systems link personnel with positions, our interviews indicate that position data do not necessarily reflect requirements or authorizations, and that vacant positions are often not reported—limiting the usefulness of the gap analysis.

A second data challenge stems from the fact that manpower requirements are driven by an organization's need to support activities, rather than by occupations. Manpower datasets, both military and civilian, reflect this focus. Although occupation codes may be available in the requirements or authorizations data, managers on the manpower side emphasize functions or activities, rather than occupations.

Centralized civilian and contractor manpower data suffer from additional challenges because, unlike military manpower, which is centrally managed at the service level, civilians and contractors are managed locally and are paid for out of the Operations and Maintenance (O&M) budget. A local command may choose to increase or decrease the number of civilians it hires, or the level of contracting support it uses, by substituting funds from one part of the O&M budget to another. As a result, data on civilian requirements are not authoritative, and data on contractor authorizations are extremely limited. To the extent that they exist, they often do not provide information on occupation or functional areas. Data calls or new reporting requirements would be needed to obtain such data.

The nature of personnel and manpower data poses challenges for workforce analyses at the occupation or functional community level within DoD, where functional communities are defined by occupation. The challenges are even greater when it comes to analyzing workforce segments that cannot be easily identified by occupation codes. Important examples in DoD include the acquisition workforce, the expeditionary workforce, and the cyber workforce. With the exception of the acquisition workforce, there is no way to identify members of these other workforce segments in a systematic way, nor it is possible to obtain data on requirements information for these groups. New data reporting requirements would be needed to identify these workforce segments in a systematic way.

Conclusions and Recommendations

Workforce analysis is an essential component of the workforce planning process. This report describes numerous approaches and specific tools that are available to help managers analyze the workforce in support of workforce planning. Each of the tools discussed in this document has strengths and weaknesses. The best tool or approach will depend on the question that needs to be addressed and the resources (data and expertise) available.

The relative costs and benefits of different workforce analysis techniques vary based on the level at which they are applied. In assessing the costs and benefits of using a particular tool or approach, it is important to recognize that workforce analysis requires resources. Two types of resources are worth highlighting: the time and resources required to collect and maintain data for workforce analysis and the capacity to analyze the data and use the analysis to inform decisions. A key question is whether the resources are available at the level at which DoD seeks to conduct workforce planning and analysis.

DoD Data Limitations May Impede Total Workforce Analysis of Functional Communities and Occupations

A centralized database that contains military, civilian, and contractor personnel and manpower data from all DoD services and agencies and that links personnel and manpower data would provide the ideal source of information for total DoD workforce planning at the occupation or functional community level. While the Defense Civilian Personnel Data System (DCPDS), the Active Duty Military Personnel Master File, and Work Experience File (WEX) are rich sources of centralized data for onboard personnel, attempts to centralize other aspects of manpower and personnel data have not been similarly successful. Moreover, options for linking manpower and workforce data—especially to analyze functional communities or occupations—are highly limited. Systematic data collection on contractor manpower and personnel and on personnel competencies and competency requirements is in its infancy.

Strategies for Addressing Data Limitations

Developing data reporting requirements to address the data limitations described above would require substantial time and effort. We provide an array of options for conducting workforce analysis at the functional community or occupation level, ranging from short-term options that can be implemented with existing data and analytic capabilities, to medium-term options that assume that the availability of systematic data on workforce competencies and the contractor workforce improves over time, to long-term options that would require substantial retooling of data systems and processes.

The limitations are rooted to a certain extent in legislative requirements regarding the management of the civilian workforce. Past experience with the development of DoD-wide systems and reporting requirements suggests that new requirements are likely to experience resistance and that the quality of data collected may be lower than expected. In the short term, with existing data, functional community managers should be able to compare counts of authorizations against counts of personnel, at least within the military services, by combining DCPDS and Active Duty Military Personnel Master File personnel data with service-level manpower datasets. We recommend that DoD consider options for supporting occupation-level analyses that are based on existing data systems and tools, including supporting the more effective use of requirements and authorizations data by workforce analysts. Also in the short term, local managers can proceed with new or ongoing data collection efforts targeting their workforces. For example, even targeted or nonsystematic exit surveys that explore the reasons behind separation could be helpful in understanding why employees in critical occupations depart. Similarly, targeted collection of competency information could be used by managers at a local level, even if there is limited capacity in the short term to roll up the data.

Over the medium term, as the availability of systematic data on workforce competencies and the contractor workforce improves over time, additional workforce analyses will become feasible. In view of the limitations with workforce demand data and the options for gathering such data, it may be valuable for DoD to build capacity for gathering needed data and conducting gap analyses at the local level. In the medium term, this would involve limited, bottom-up analysis focused on high-priority mission critical occupations (MCOs) or functional areas. Bottom-up analyses can be time-consuming and potentially costly but may be better able to capture qualitative insights from local managers. A survey tool could be used to identify gaps among civilian, military, and contractor employees performing high-priority functions. These reported gaps could be aggregated across activities. Such targeted, qualitative surveys may be particularly useful in the context of cross-cutting workforces, such as the cyber or expeditionary workforces, that cannot be easily identified in the personnel or requirements data using occupation codes or other data codes.

Over the long term, DoD can consider the data requirements for supporting an ideal top-down analysis of manpower gaps. Such analysis would require information about supply and demand that could be appropriately linked by either function or occupation for all workforce segments (military, civilian, and contractor). The scope and the potential expense of such an ambitious data collection effort are daunting, and several notable barriers challenge the potential viability of a gold standard top-down analysis. A logistical challenge is creating an incentive for managers to report information regularly and completely.

An alternative and potentially more feasible recommendation for the long term would be to build capacity for workforce analysis at the local level. Just as with specialized qualitative questionnaires for high-interest groups in the medium term, in the long term more standardized qualitative questions may be rolled out to all local offices/commands concerning what gaps exist. The determination of what constitutes the "local" level depends on the locus at which dollar budgets are allocated and reshuffled across specific positions. For example, in the Air Force, the major commands serve as the local level, or the business unit level, determining the number of contractors and civilians to hire. Furthermore, it would be worthwhile for OPM to work with other offices in DoD in arriving at more productive levels of analysis, rather than occupation. More flexibility can be achieved by keeping functions more general than a specific MCO.

In making this recommendation, our point is not that occupations or functional communities should not be analyzed at the DoD-wide level. However, given the challenges with requirements data, it may be more effective to compare supply and demand at a local level and then to aggregate the information about gaps to the DoD-wide level to present an overall picture of workforce health in a particular occupation. Performing an initial analysis using the central manpower systems, and using data calls when needed to investigate potentially large or growing gaps, would help to balance the need to collect information against the goal of minimizing reporting requirements.

Our review suggests that DoD has made substantial progress in collecting data on competencies and on the contractor workforce, but it remains unclear whether the data required to support gap analyses for occupations or functional communities that include contractors or competencies will be feasible to collect. Here again, a more feasible course of action would be to tap available data sets and supplement that information with gap analyses conducted at more local levels, relying on a DoD-wide data call only when absolutely necessary.

Acknowledgments

The authors would like to thank Nick Byone, Frank Camm, Ray Conley, Larry Hanser, Gary Massey, Albert Robbert, and Peter Schirmer for sharing their experiences with various data systems within DoD. We are also indebted to Garry Shafovaloff, Keith Lowe, Stephen Chesley, and Jane Datta for their insightful discussions regarding their use of data. The authors would also like to thank Lindsay Daugherty, who provided additional support in examining potential data sources, and Ken Kuhn, who contributed to the discussion of optimization modeling. Al Robbert at RAND and Dan L. Ward at the MITRE Corporation provided valuable reviews. Any remaining errors are the responsibility of the authors.

Abbreviations

AF/A1M	Air Force Directorate of Manpower, Organization, and Resources
AFMC	Air Force Material Command
AFPC	Air Force Personnel Center
AFSC	Air Force Special Code
AMSAA	Army Material Systems Analysis Activity
ARMA	autoregressive moving average
ASCAR	accession supply costing and requirements
ASU	Acquisition/Sustainment Unit
AVAIL	Available Labor Force
AW	acquisition workforce
BRAC	Base Closure and Realignment Commission
CIVFORS	Civilian Forecasting System
CME	contractor manpower equivalent
CMIS	Corporate Management Information System
CMRA	Contractor Manpower Reporting Application
CSRS	Civil Service Retirement System

DASD (CPP)	Deputy Assistant Secretary of Defense for Civilian Personnel Policy
DCAMIS	DoD Commercial Activities Management Information System
DCPAS-SHCPD	Defense Civilian Personnel Advisory Service, Strategic Human Capital Planning Division
DCPDS	Defense Civilian Personnel Data System
DLA	Defense Logistics Agency
DMDC	Defense Manpower Data Center
DoD	U.S. Department of Defense
eCMRA	enterprise-wide Contractor Manpower Reporting Application
ELIM-COMPLIP	Enlisted Loss Inventory Model—Computation of Manpower Programs Using Linear Programming
EX	Electronic Combat Coordinator
FC	functional community
FERS	Federal Employees Retirement System
FMS	Force Management System
FPDS-NG	Federal Procurement Data System—Next Generation
FTE	full-time equivalent
FY	fiscal year
GAO	Government Accountability Office
GTO	Generating Force-to-Operator

HQ ACPERS	Army Civilian Personnel System
HR	human resources
HRC	Human Resource Command
IMCOM	U.S. Army Installation Management Command
IT	information technology
IWAPM	Integrated Workforce Analysis and Planning Model
LOGCAP	Logistics Civil Augmentation Program
MAF	manpower availability factor
MAJCOM	major command
MCM	Military Career Model
MCO	mission critical occupation
MCTFS	Marine Corps Total Force System
MEP	Management Engineering Program
MEPCOM	Military Enlistment Processing Command
MilPDS	Air Force Military Personnel Data System
MOS	Military Occupation Specialty
MPES	Manning Programming and Execution System
NASA	National Aeronautics and Space Administration
NDAA	National Defense Authorization Act
NETCOM	U.S. Army Network Enterprise Technology Command
NGT	nominal group technique
NIPRNet	Nonsecure Internet Protocol Router Network

O&M	Operations and Maintenance
OPM	Office of Personnel Management
OSD	Office of the Secretary of Defense
OUSD (AT&L)	Office of the Under Secretary of Defense for Acquisition, Technology, and Logistics
OUSD (P&R)	Office of the Under Secretary of Defense for Personnel and Readiness
PLFA	primary level field activities
PWAM	Procurement Workload Analysis Model
RCMOP	Requirements-Driven Cost-Based Optimization
SACOM	Sustainment and Acquisition Composite Model
SAMAS	Structure and Manpower Allocation System
SEI	Special Expertise Identifier
SES	Senior Executive Service
SIPRNet	Secret Internet Protocol Router Network
STEM	science, technology, engineering, and mathematics
TAA	Total Army Analysis
TAADS	Army Authorization Document System
TFMMS	Total Force Manpower Management System
THRMIS	Total Human Resource Managers' Information System
TTP	time to produce
UIC	unit identification code

UMD	Unit Manpower Document
USMIRS	U.S. MEPCOM [Military Enlistment Processing Command] Information Resource System
WAM	workload assessment model
WEX	Work Experience File
WYE	work-year equivalent
YORE	years relative to retirement eligibility

CHAPTER ONE

Introduction

Under 10 U.S.C. 115b (National Defense Authorization Act [NDAA] Fiscal Year [FY] 2010, Section 1108), the Office of the Under Secretary of Defense for Personnel and Readiness (OUSD [P&R]) has responsibility for developing and implementing the Department of Defense's (DoD's) strategic workforce plan, in consultation with the Office of the Under Secretary of Defense for Acquisition, Technology, and Logistics (OUSD [AT&L]). Statutory requirements added in the FY 2010 NDAA require that DoD's strategic workforce plan address a set of requirements related to the overall civilian workforce, the senior leader workforce, and the acquisition workforce. An audit conducted by the U.S. Government Accountability Office (GAO) reviewing the 2013–2018 Strategic Workforce Plan concluded that the DoD plan had made progress toward, but had not fully addressed, the legislative requirements that pertain to planning for the overall civilian workforce (GAO, 2014). In keeping with the legislative requirements, DoD seeks to accelerate improvements to the department's workforce data, forecasting methods, tools, and analysis to develop a comprehensive, measurable planning process that drives strategic human capital management decisions within the Total Force construct. In support of these efforts, DoD seeks to improve upon the tools available to analyze the civilian workforce DoD-wide and enhance its strategy for capturing and using data on the DoD-wide workforce, including military, civilian, and contractor employees.

Workforce Gap Analysis Is a Key Aspect of the Workforce Planning Process

Workforce planning can be defined as having the "right number of people with the right set of skills and competencies in the right job at the right time" (Vernez et al., 2007). The basic goal is to close any gaps between the human resources that an organization needs to carry out its mission (demand) and the human resources it has (supply). Effective workforce planning not only aids organizations in using resources effectively and ensuring that the organization has the staff needed to accomplish its objectives. It also can help organizations identify and address workforce risks. Workforce risks are workforce issues that could prevent an organization from achieving its aims (Australian Public Service Commission, 2012, p. 3).

As shown in Figure 1.1, the workforce planning process may be divided into six major steps (adapted from Office of Personnel Management [OPM] guidance [OPM, "OPM's Workforce Planning Model," undated]):

1. **Set strategic direction.** Identify the ways in which the organization's long-term and short-term goals might affect workforce planning. This is often accomplished through an *environmental scan*, in which an organization identifies internal drivers (such as changes in the organization's mission) and external drivers (such as economic conditions) that may affect the organization's human resource needs and gathers high-level information about these drivers.

2a. **Determine workforce supply.** Determine what the current workforce looks like and how it is likely to evolve over time based on current trends, existing personnel policies and practices, and drivers identified in Step 1. Workforce supply projection usually begins with analyzing human resources data to understand the historical patterns of worker separation, hiring, transfers, promotions, and other key activities. Historical patterns are then projected into the future, using one of a variety of techniques, to arrive at future workforce supply projections.

Figure 1.1
Overview of the Workforce Planning Process

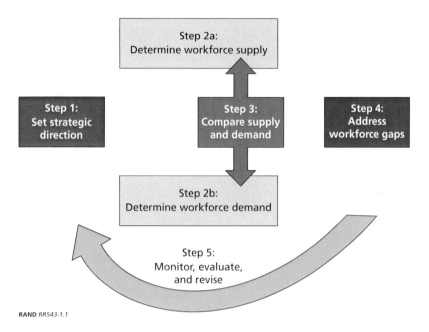

RAND *RR543-1.1*

Projections may take into account anticipated changes in worker behavior, human resource policies, or other conditions that are likely to make future patterns deviate from historical patterns.

2b. **Determine workforce demand.** Use information about current and projected future workload, as well as drivers identified in Step 1, to project what future workforce requirements will be. Workforce demand projection can take multiple forms, but typically involves three stages: (1) Assess current workload and workforce productivity, (2) project workload into the future, and (3) project future productivity and apply to future workload in order to derive future workforce size.

3. **Compare the demand with the supply.** Identify gaps between supply (the projected future workforce from Step 2a) and demand (the desired future workforce from Step 2b). Gaps are not lim-

ited strictly to a difference between the numerical estimates of workforce supply and demand; they can also be inferred from assessments of organizational effectiveness and assessments of workforce stress. A workforce gap can be manifested in terms of low effectiveness or high stress.

4. **Develop and implement an action plan.** Identify and implement strategies to close gaps between supply and demand that were identified in Step 3.

5. **Monitor, evaluate, and revise.** Monitor progress toward the goals established in the action plan, and revise strategies as needed.

Prior research suggests that workforce planning in DoD is more complicated than this simple framework would suggest because the activities can occur at different levels of the organization (Gates et al., 2006). Analyses conducted at different organizational levels in support of workforce planning serve different purposes. Managers may need to access different data and employ different analytical approaches, depending on their objectives.

Purpose

This report provides a review of analytical approaches used in the private sector and in government organizations for tackling Steps 2a and 2b of the workforce planning process described above—namely, determining workforce supply and demand. We assess the feasibility and usefulness of applying the methods described here given the resources available to support workforce analysis within DoD, including data availability. We consider what improvements to data or other supports might be effective in promoting the use of these analytical tools.

Approach

To achieve the purpose of this report, we engaged in two key research tasks:

1. We reviewed approaches to workforce supply and demand analysis.
2. We reviewed existing data to support workforce demand and supply analysis within DoD.

We describe our approach to each task in turn.

Review of Approaches to Workforce Supply and Demand Analysis

We began by identifying articles on workforce supply and demand determination in the academic literature, government publications, and human resources journals and texts. On the supply side, articles were identified through targeted searches of the workforce literature using the EBSCO Host and Google Scholar search engines. A variety of terms were used to make the review as exhaustive as possible. Two initial searches provided a broad overview of the literature:

- (workforce OR labor OR manpower OR human resources) AND (forecast OR planning OR model OR projection)
- workforce planning OR labor supply OR manpower AND forecasting.

This overview helped generate more focused keywords for later searches, which included the following terms:

- succession planning workforce model
- workforce model human capital management
- public sector workforce planning
- workforce planning talent management
- strategic human capital management workforce model
- government workforce planning model
- workforce succession planning

- workforce planning employment gap
- strategic human capital management.

The objective of these focused searches was to find documents that included some discussion of workforce planning and labor supply, although special attention was paid to articles that outlined working models. For each search, the titles and abstracts of at least the top 50 results were examined, and if the search criteria were met, the papers were reviewed more thoroughly.

The following search was also used to examine the literature on four specific types of workforce models:

- workforce planning AND (Markov chain model OR supply chain model OR optimization model OR simulation model).

Our search of the literature identified several specific tools that are used for workforce supply and demand planning. In addition, we used Google searches to identify commercial software tools. Several keywords were used:

- strategic workforce planning software
- workforce planning software
- succession planning software.

Nine companies that produce software used in workforce planning were identified:

- ClickSoftware
- Human Capital Management Institute
- Integrated Workforce Analysis and Planning Model
- PeopleFluent
- Oracle PeopleSoft
- PeopleSteme
- SAS Workforce Planning and Analytics for Government
- WorkDay
- WorkPlace.

Information on these systems was collected from company websites, demos, and promotional materials. Based on a preliminary scan of available information, we identified several systems that warranted further investigation. We contacted representatives from ClickSoftware, Human Capital Management Institute, SAS, and WorkDay by phone. During these calls, we asked vendor representatives for additional information about their systems' capabilities and methodologies for creating supply and demand forecasts. Information about the software systems that appear to be most appropriate is included in Chapter Five of this report.

The literature search on the demand side proceeded down two primary avenues. First, initial searches of academic and business databases (e.g., Business Source Premier) were conducted using the following search terms: (workforce OR human resource OR manpower OR labor) AND (demand OR projection OR forecast OR planning OR model). This led us to human resources journals for general explanations and overviews of various demand projection techniques. Many such articles included the following terms:

- workforce demand forecasting
- human resource planning
- workforce projection
- workforce planning.

We identified a specialized quarterly journal titled *People & Strategy* (formerly *Human Resource Planning*), which is published by an educational association, HR People & Strategy (formerly the Human Resource Planning Society). Members of the association hold academic, consulting, and business positions, and the association publishes research reports and holds conferences on best practices in strategic human resource management.

A second avenue involved a search for examples and applications of demand forecasting over a range of workforce types, as categorized below:

- U.S. DoD workforce
  - services (e.g., Air Force, Army)
  - acquisition workforce
- U.S. government
  - non-DoD federal agencies
- private sector organizations or industries
  - health care workforce (physicians, nurses)
  - education workforce (teachers).

Information and documentation on specific demand models were solicited from the Defense Technical Information Center, acquisition research symposium reports, and RAND researchers with direct experience working on and reviewing demand models for various workforces. This avenue was especially helpful in generating detailed profiles of individual models.

Review of Workforce Data Resources in DoD

Given the vast and decentralized nature of data collection and storage in DoD, we took a top-down approach to identifying key data systems for our review. We began by examining major, DoD-wide data systems, and then moved down to the level of the services and large agencies. We identified key sources through a variety of means, including searching DoD-wide and service-specific documents that provide guidance regarding requirements determination; examining the lists of data systems identified by the manpower and personnel offices at individual services and agencies; investigating publicly available codebooks for service-specific data systems; and speaking with researchers and data users familiar with service-specific DoD data sources and requirements generation processes.

Data on military personnel in DoD—particularly when it comes to authorizations—tend to be more detailed and easily available than data on civilian personnel and contractors. Therefore, we focused our efforts on identifying civilian and contractor data systems, although we did collect basic information about the military data contained within those systems as well. For each system, we attempted to ascertain whether the data included military, civilian, or contractor inventories or requirements. We also paid particular attention to whether the data contained any variables that could be used in determining competency requirements or levels.

Overview of Report

Chapter Two of this report provides an overview of the key issues and choices involved in specifying and projecting workforce supply and demand. Chapters Three and Four delve into a more detailed analysis of the methods that can be used to project future supply and demand, respectively. In Chapter Five, we discuss some variables that are commonly used in supply and demand analysis and provide an overview of the main types of data sources used in supply and demand analysis. We also provide a detailed analysis of the availability of data sources within DoD. In Chapter Six, we discuss the key data challenges facing DoD. Chapter Seven offers conclusions and recommendations.

CHAPTER TWO

Overview of Supply and Demand Modeling Approaches

When approaching workforce supply and demand analysis, managers are faced with critical choices about the scope of analysis, the level of aggregation, the type of projection techniques that will be used, the time period over which historical analysis of projections will be conducted, and the data sources to be used. In this chapter, we describe the nature of these choices, which affect both supply and demand analysis, laying the groundwork for a more targeted discussion of modeling approaches in Chapters Three and Four.

Scope of Analysis

Determining the scope of the analysis involves several decisions, including what subpopulations of the workforce will be analyzed, what aspects of the workforce (for example, number of workers, worker characteristics) will be covered, and whether external labor supply will be examined. Here we discuss some of the factors that can be used to determine the appropriate scope of analysis.

Organization-Wide Versus Subpopulation Analysis
A basic choice facing any workforce modeler is whether to consider the whole organization or to limit the analysis to one or more subpopulations. The appropriate scope of the analysis will be influenced by the nature of the question the analysis is intended to inform. Organization-

11

wide modeling may be appropriate as part of a broader human resources strategy, while focusing on key subpopulations may be more appropriate when managers are concerned about recruiting or retaining people with specific skill sets or other characteristics (Premier's Department of New South Wales, 2003). Cost and time factors may also play a role. Organization-wide modeling is likely to require more resources. If an organization-wide analysis is selected, the modeling may still be done at a more disaggregated level and can be rolled up to create aggregate estimates; issues involved in determining the appropriate *level* (rather than the *scope*) of analysis are discussed in the next section.

A subpopulation may be defined in a number of ways, involving employees in a particular occupation, with a particular degree or skill set, performing a particular function, or holding certain types of positions. For example, workforce planners who are concerned about recruiting and retaining employees with technical skills may focus on a subpopulation with science, technology, engineering, and mathematics (STEM) degrees. Another common choice is to focus workforce planning on upper-level management positions; organizations may attempt to identify likely vacancies in high-level positions and to identify and train potential employees who could fill such vacancies (Bulmash, Chhinzer, and Speers, 2010).

In DoD, these choices are of particular relevance because the overall workforce is extremely large and there are so many possible subpopulations. Subpopulations may be defined by occupation, by occupational groupings, by service or agency, by subunits of a service or agency, by geographic area, by installation, or by a combination of these categories.

Number of Workers Versus Worker Characteristics

Most workforce projection models focus on a basic measure: number of workers. While this is a necessary first step, organizational goals may require an analysis of additional measures. Even if the total projected supply of workers equals the total projected demand, there may be a deficit of workers with certain skills or characteristics and a surplus of workers with others.

Workforce managers in DoD and elsewhere have been working to identify workforce competencies. A competency can be defined as "a set of behaviors that encompass skills, knowledge, abilities, and personal attributes, that taken together, are critical to successful work accomplishment" (Bulmash, Chhinzer, and Speers, 2010, p. 36). For example, Masi et al. (2009) developed a competency model for the Human Resource Command (HRC) in which they identified required competencies for each position, as well as the level of proficiency required for each competency (exposure, experience, or expertise). Identifying these requirements can assist managers in matching employees with the positions for which they are fitted and in better targeting their external recruiting efforts. The National Aeronautics and Space Administration's (NASA's) workforce planning model also incorporates competencies; the model is designed to identify competency shortages and plan workforce decisions accordingly. Personnel with critical competencies receive priority in hiring and are less likely to be forced to leave. The competencies required for each position are updated annually, while the competencies of staff are updated as soon as a change is made (NASA, 2008).

Other worker characteristics may also be considered. As discussed above, organizations such as DoD may choose to focus on the supply and demand of workers with specific types of educational attainment, such as STEM degrees. An organization interested in promoting workforce diversity may project the mix of workers by gender, race, or ethnicity. The appropriate mix of military, civilian, and contractor personnel may also be of interest to DoD (Vernez et al., 2007).

Given the potentially large amount of information required to estimate workforce supply and demand by worker characteristics, it may be desirable to conduct organization-wide estimates for the number of workers and to focus on worker characteristics only in key cases. Vernez et al. (2007) recommended that the Air Force Material Command (AFMC) project the required number of workers for each of its core business units, but that competency requirements only be determined for core occupations.

Each of the analysis techniques described below can incorporate worker characteristics in various ways. One option is to conduct the analysis separately for workers with specific characteristics; this option is discussed in more detail in the next section, which deals with levels of analysis. Another option is to incorporate information about worker characteristics, skills, educational attainment, or other dimensions into the projection of supply or demand using regression or other techniques, which are briefly reviewed later in this chapter and are discussed in more detail in Chapters Three and Four.

Internal Versus External Workforce

This choice pertains to supply rather than demand models. Most supply models focus on "internal supply" forecasting: They describe and project the behavior of current employees. To the extent that new employees are needed, these models tend to assume that qualified new hires can be found. However, it may also be important to consider characteristics of the potential pool of labor, particularly when the supply projection assumes that new employees with specific skills, or in specific regions, can be found. In Chapter Three, we discuss an example of such "external supply" analysis for the Army HRC during its relocation to Fort Knox (Masi et al., 2009).

Level of Aggregation

Once the scope has been established, the manager must decide the *level of aggregation* at which information should be gathered and analyses should be conducted. Suppose the goal is to create projections for the information technology (IT) workforce in DoD. One option would be to perform projections for all IT workers in DoD as a whole. Alternatively, projections could be undertaken for smaller subpopulations within the IT workforce—such as IT workers within the Army, Navy, Air Force, and Office of the Secretary of Defense (OSD), separately—and then aggregated to develop an estimate for the DoD-wide IT workforce.

A number of considerations factor into the decision about the level at which to conduct workforce analysis. First, the size and heterogeneity of the workforce to be analyzed should be considered, with attention devoted to the question of which differences in characteristics might be expected to result in different workforce behavior or outcomes. Analysts will want to model worker flows for individual groups where they expect behavior to vary significantly across groups. For example, previous RAND research has found that in the Navy's acquisition workforce, retention rates vary by career field and education level (Gates et al., 2009). Physician supply models typically account for the projected share of female physicians, as female physicians tend to enter different specialties, work different hours, and exhibit different retirement patterns than male physicians (see, for example, U.S. Department of Health and Human Services, 2008). Differences across geographic regions or occupations may be masked if too high a level is selected; if one location has a surplus of workers but another has a deficit, analyzing workforce supply and demand at a level that aggregates across the two locations will miss both the surplus and the deficit (Bechet, 1994). Similarly, a high-level view may miss the distinctions between occupations; a "technical specialist" may require fundamentally different skills in different offices within the same organization (Bechet, 2008). In contrast, if the workforce in question is homogeneous, then worker behavior and requirements are less likely to vary across different groups of workers, and the analysis may be conducted at a more aggregate level.

A related issue concerns the size of the workforce: For a small organization, it may be necessary to conduct quantitative modeling at a high level, as small sample sizes can pose challenges for statistical analysis. The commonly used stock-and-flow supply model, which models behavior for aggregate groups of employees rather than for individuals, may not be appropriate for groups of fewer than 100 employees (Edwards, 1983).

Second, the appropriate level of aggregation depends on who will be using the results of the analysis and for what purpose. Bechet (2008) proposes that workforce plans be created "at the same level as [the] probable solution." Along these lines, Emmerichs, Marcum, and Robbert (2004) suggest that workforce analysis is most relevant for business unit managers, who are engaged in workforce planning efforts on a regular basis in order to ensure the business unit's ability to achieve its outcomes. A specific example is provided by Vernez et al. (2007) in their report on workforce planning in AFMC. They note that the AFMC consists of "quasi-independent business units" that are responsible for different products at different stages of development. Each unit's workload (and therefore its workforce requirements) ebbs and flows at different times. Thus, they recommend that the AFMC conduct workforce planning at the business unit level.

However, there are many reasons why other types of managers, such as those at the occupation, career-field, or command levels, may be engaged in workforce analysis and planning. Some of these levels might be aggregations of several business units. Other levels may be cross-cutting. For example, a human resources manager who is responsible for a particular occupational group may be interested in an analysis of that occupation. In that case, Bechet (2008) suggests that a separate model of workers in the cross-cutting occupation be developed. It is common for organizations to conduct workforce analysis by occupation or specialization within an occupation, particularly when a worker in one group cannot be easily substituted for a worker in another group. Projections of physician supply and demand typically estimate overall numbers, as well as supply and demand for each specialty (see, for example, Dill and Salsberg, 2008; U.S. Department of Health and Human Services, 2008). Breaking down the analysis by specialty is important in this context, as the projected imbalance between supply and demand varies widely between specialties; for example, a national projection suggests a slight surplus in primary care physicians by 2020 but a large deficit in surgical specialties (U.S. Department of Health and Human Services, 2008).

Third, the cost and time requirements of conducting the workforce analysis exercise at a given level should be taken into account. If, for example, the goal is to create an organization-wide estimate of supply or demand, then projections may be made either at the overall, organization-wide level or at suborganizational levels and then rolled up. To the extent that a quantitative model, drawing on existing data, is used, the additional cost associated with conducting the analysis at a disaggregated level may be fairly minor. A number of supply projection software tools, which are discussed in more detail in Chapters Three and Five, allow the user to project supply at various levels, as well as at an aggregate level, fairly easily. The main additional cost, in this case, would involve the time required to analyze the results for subpopulations, as well as for the main population.

The availability of information needed to address different stages of the workforce planning and analysis process may vary at different levels of the organization. If the required data do not already exist at the desired subpopulation level and if gathering and analyzing those data will be costly, then the organization must weigh the costs of such data collection against the potential benefits of a disaggregated analysis, which may not be sufficient to justify the increased cost or time. For example, to determine workload requirements, many contracting organizations estimate the relationship between workload and staffing levels in each office and then project future staffing needs based on future workload. The data needed to conduct this type of analysis— staffing levels and workloads—typically exist. Suppose, however, that a manager wishes to project staffing requirements by occupation as well as by office, and that the organization does not currently collect information about occupation. The cost of modifying the data-gathering process to classify employees by occupation would need to be weighed against the incremental benefit of projecting staffing requirements by occupation.

While work requirements or overall workforce shaping goals may be determined at relatively high levels, monitoring the current workforce and identifying specific workforce needs are often performed at lower levels and with a higher level of detail. Within NASA, for example, agency management oversees the planning process and makes decisions about internal versus external labor sourcing; below this level, mission directorates define work requirements and distribute funding; and, finally, centers monitor their workforces and define workforce requirements for work that they are assigned. Similarly, Vernez et al. (2007) recommend identifying key changes that may affect workforce requirements at the business unit level but identifying workforce requirements to support these changes at a lower level of line and functional managers. They note that for the purpose of estimating future workforce competency requirements, "there is no alternative but to rely on the expert judgment of those who are close enough to the work that has to be done but high enough in the organization to have a strategic view. In our experience, this is found at the level of line and functional managers" (p. 22). The levels at which information should be gathered will be specific to each situation and will depend on the availability of data, as well as on more qualitative issues, such as managers' familiarity with workforce requirements.

Types of Projection Techniques

Projections or forecasts of future workforce supply and demand are an important feature of workforce supply and demand analysis. There are two basic types of techniques used for workforce projection: quantitative and qualitative. A combination of both quantitative and qualitative techniques may provide the best assessment of the current and projected workforce. For example, supply projections commonly rely on quantitative, human resources data to estimate the expected retirement rate for groups of employees. To the extent that managers would like to understand whether future retention rates will be similar to historical retention rates, it may be necessary to collect qualitative data on reasons for separation.

In this section, we present an overview of several choices that must be made when using quantitative and qualitative projection techniques. Details of individual techniques are provided in Chapters Three and Four, and Chapter Five describes some specific software and other tools.

Quantitative Projections

Quantitative projections typically involve projecting historical patterns into the future. In practice, quantitative techniques are more commonly used by larger organizations[1] (Premier's Department of

---

[1]   Quantitative manpower planning has progressively evolved over the last several decades, particularly with the growth of data availability and computational resources. See Vajda (1978) for an early treatment of quanitative modeling, and Ward, Tripp, and Maki (2013) for an overview of the history of workforce planning.

New South Wales, 2003). Developing a quantitative projection model involves several choices, which are outlined below.

Deterministic Versus Stochastic Projections

Deterministic projections provide an estimate of the future number of workers (either supplied or demanded) but do not take into account the statistical uncertainty associated with this estimate. Supply projections typically rely on stock-and-flow models, which (in their basic form) are deterministic. A stock-and-flow model has several benefits:

- It mimics the natural "aging" process of the workforce.
- It allows different cohorts to exhibit different retention and recruiting patterns.
- The underlying mechanism is fairly transparent.

However, it provides only a single number for estimated workforce size, rather than an estimated range, and thus may make estimates appear to be more accurate than they are.

Stochastic models, such as regression models, can explicitly account for statistical uncertainty. They provide not only a single, best estimate of workforce size, but also a confidence interval indicating a likely range. Regression models are more commonly used in forecasting demand, but a variety of stochastic tools, including regression techniques, have also been incorporated into stock-and-flow supply models.

Regardless of whether deterministic or stochastic models are used, users should be aware that results are highly dependent on the underlying assumptions. In the case of deterministic, stock-and-flow models, assumptions about historical flow rates are critical. One potential method for creating a range of estimates would be to vary the underlying assumptions about flow rates. In the case of regression methods, the critical assumption is that historical trends, as well as historical relationships between worker supply or demand and key factors driving supply or demand, will continue into the future.

Descriptive Versus Optimization Models

"Descriptive" models can project historical trends into the future and can also be used to answer "what if" questions by allowing users to change assumed parameters. For example, one version of the RAND Inventory Model projects future worker supply based on historical new-hire and separation rates. The model also allows users to change new-hire and separation rates, thus asking such questions as "What would projected workforce supply be if there were a hiring freeze?" However, this model does not identify the "best" hiring policy; rather, it takes as given the policies selected by users, and projects future workforce size based on those policies.

In contrast, optimization models maximize (or minimize) an objective function given a set of constraints. For example, such a model may identify feasible hiring policies that minimize cost. The benefit of using optimization models is that such models can help users to identify specific policies that can efficiently achieve their objectives. Drawbacks include the complexity of optimization models, coupled with the fact that few manpower planners have training in optimization techniques. In addition, optimization models tend to focus on one objective, whereas planners often have several, potentially competing objectives.[2]

Analytic Versus Simulation Techniques

Analytic models are those for which solutions can be calculated using mathematical methods. Simulation models typically cannot be solved in this way; instead, the equations that govern the model are implemented in a spreadsheet or programming language, which proceeds through the model until an acceptable solution is reached numerically. An advantage of simulation models is that they allow users to calculate workforce projections even in cases where the underlying mathematical relationships are so complex that no analytic solution is possible. For example, a manager may wish to create a model that moves workers into the next year of service automatically but only assigns them to higher grades when positions are available. Developing an analytical model for this type of system would be challenging, but creating a computer program that simulates the behavior of the system by fol-

---

[2] In Chapter Three, we discuss optimization techniques that do address multiple objectives, although they add complexity and can be highly sensitive to the "weight" assigned to each objective.

lowing a sequence of rules regarding separation, promotion, and hiring would be relatively simple (Bartholomew and Forbes, 1979). Two key disadvantages of simulation models are potentially high computational and time costs (Wang, 2005).

Aggregate Versus Agent-Based Models

Aggregate models are based on the behavior of certain groups of employees. Employees are typically divided into groups of people who might be expected to exhibit reasonably similar behavior. For example, the RAND Inventory Model divides employees into cells based on years remaining until retirement eligibility, since retirement eligibility is one of the strongest predictors of separation. In other contexts, such characteristics as geographic location, gender, or position may be more salient. An aggregate model counts the number of individuals in a particular cell and assigns transition rates to each cell. For instance, there might be ten employees who are 15 years away from retirement, with an estimated separation rate of 10 percent; thus, next year the model would estimate that one out of the ten employees would separate.

In contrast, agent-based models represent individual workers who make decisions in accordance with certain rules. Their actions may be affected by their individual characteristics, by their environment, or by other agents in the model (Better et al., 2013). Agent-based models are stochastic; instead of a transition rate, each employee has transition probabilities.[3] In the example above, each of the ten employees who are 15 years away from retirement would have a 10-percent chance of leaving. Those transition probabilities may be shaped by the external environment (for example, a separation incentive). Agent-based models have high computational costs, as they require the simulation of decisions and interactions of many individuals, which can then be aggregated. However, they allow behavior to be modeled based on a richer set of individual characteristics than do aggregated models.

---

[3] Aggregate models can also be stochastic but are often deterministic.

Qualitative Projections

In this section, we review some of the key decisions that relate to qualitative projection techniques. While the techniques discussed below may be applied to both supply and demand projections, our review of the literature indicated that qualitative techniques are more commonly used in projecting demand.

Number of Scenarios

Planners often develop multiple "scenarios" and then project future worker supply or demand under each scenario. Scenarios can be defined as "sets of individual changes that are most likely to occur in concert" (Vernez et al., 2007, p. 21). When using quantitative models, users can easily consider alternative scenarios by changing model inputs and quickly generating revised projections. For example, the RAND Inventory Model allows users to compare the default scenario, in which historical hiring and separation rates continue into the future, with alternative scenarios, such as a reduction in hiring or an increase in voluntary separations, simply by changing input numbers in a spreadsheet.

In contrast, many qualitative models depend on eliciting expert or manager opinion about how conditions will change in the future in order to craft a few key scenarios. In this case, a more careful decision must be made about how many scenarios to develop, as expert consensus must be obtained for each scenario, and end users cannot simply add new scenarios at will. Rather, the development of specific scenarios should be part of the elicitation of expert ideas.

Method of Eliciting Expert or Manager Opinions

As discussed above, scenarios for workforce projections (particularly for demand) are often developed by soliciting expert opinion. The Delphi method, originally developed by RAND, is commonly used for this purpose (Dalkey and Helmer-Hirschberg, 1962). The Delphi method involves eliciting opinions from several experts about potential changes that would affect the workforce (forecasts); summarizing all expert opinions and circulating them to the group of experts, so that they can review the summary and adjust their forecasts, if desired; and iterating through this process until results converge (Vernez et al., 2007).

During the Delphi process, experts do not meet to discuss their projections. The rationale for this restriction is to encourage independent thought and to avoid direct confrontation among experts, which may discourage independent thought and novel ideas (Dalkey and Helmer-Hirschberg, 1962).

Another technique, also involving arm's-length data collection, is a survey of experts or managers. This technique is likely to be more cost-effective in collecting opinions from a large number of people than the Delphi technique. However, it does not permit respondents to reach a consensus.

In contrast with the Delphi method and the use of surveys, the nominal group technique (NGT) encourages face-to-face meetings among participants. It involves several steps during which experts develop their opinions independently, present them to the group, discuss their estimates, and then rank all estimates (Delbecq and Van de Ven, 1971; Bulmash, Chhinzer, and Speers, 2010). A less formal, face-to-face interaction could involve focus groups or meetings.

The appropriate method for gathering opinions will depend heavily on the nature of the organization and the specific information to be gathered. Multiple methods may also be combined. For example, the Delphi or NGT method may be used to develop expert consensus about key scenarios. Surveys may then be sent to line managers that show them the potential scenarios and ask how they expect their workload requirements to change under each scenario (Vernez et al., 2007).

Time Period

Perspectives differ on the appropriate time horizon for conducting supply and demand forecasts. If the selected time period is too short, then there may not be sufficient time for the workforce to change substantially. The longer the time period selected, the more likely it is that major, unanticipated external factors may shift during that period, thus making accurate predictions difficult (Vernez et al., 2007). Supply projection methods have been shown to become less accurate as their projections move farther out into the future (O'Brien-Pallas et al., 2001).

The appropriate timeline will differ across organizations, depending on the nature of the workforce, the workload drivers, and the types of external factors that typically affect supply or demand. Our review of the literature suggests a wide range of planning horizons, ranging from less than one year up to 20 years.

One reason for this broad range of time horizons is that organizations use different planning horizons for different types of workforce planning exercises. If the goal is to identify which employees to promote for positions that are expected to become available, a short horizon may be sufficient. A longer time horizon (on the order of three to six years) may be more appropriate for decisions that require planning, such as recruiting or training employees with specific skills or succession planning for key management positions (Bulmash, Chhinzer, and Speers, 2010). For example, NASA employs "operational" workforce planning to assign the current workforce to work requirements within the next year, "programmatic" workforce planning to match the workforce to work requirements in the two- to six-year time frame, and "strategic" workforce planning to identify the workforce needed to carry out NASA's goals (NASA, 2008). Similarly, the Australian Public Service Commission (2011) suggests a 12- to 18-month period for operational planning and a three- to five-year period for strategic planning.

Longer-term planning is also more likely to be led by higher levels of management. NASA notes that senior leaders are the key decisionmakers for its strategic planning, midlevel managers (agency and center leaders and program managers) are key decisionmakers in programmatic planning, and lower-level managers (center line and project managers) and human capital representatives are key decisionmakers in operational planning (NASA, 2008).

Summary

Table 2.1 summarizes the key considerations involved in each of the choices discussed above. In the following two chapters, we delve into one of the choices—projection technique—in more detail.

Table 2.1
Key Considerations for Workforce Planners

Choice Area	Key Considerations
Scope	• How much of the workforce to analyze • Whether to analyze subpopulations and, if so, which ones • Whether to analyze only the number of workers or other characteristics as well • Whether to consider workers outside the organization
Level of aggregation	• How large and heterogeneous the workforce is • Whether it is possible to generalize across workers within a level of aggregation • How many workers there are at a given level • At what level questions need to be answered to address strategic questions • Cost associated with conducting workforce analysis at a particular level
Type of projection technique	Quantitative • Deterministic models vs. stochastic models • Descriptive models vs. optimization models • Analytic techniques vs. simulation techniques • Aggregate models vs. agent-based models Qualitative • Number of scenarios • Method for gathering information
Time period for forecasting	• Longer time periods are used for organization-wide strategic planning; shorter time periods are used for tactical planning at the business unit level

CHAPTER THREE

Supply Models: Issues and Options

In this chapter, we discuss specific options available for modeling worker supply. We begin by providing an overview of the types of models that are typically used for supply modeling and discussing the advantages and disadvantages of each model. We then discuss several additional aspects to be considered in supply modeling.

Types of Models

Stock-and-Flow Models

The most commonly used supply model is a stock-and-flow model. A stock-and-flow model begins with the *stock* of workers in a particular year and then uses estimates of their *flows* to project future stocks. Worker flows may include gains into the organization (new hires), losses from the organization (retirements, as well as voluntary and involuntary separations), and movements within the organization (for example, promotion to a new position, switch to another occupation, or relocation to another region).

There are two major categories of stock-and-flow models: "push" and "pull" models. A push model (often called a Markov model) moves workers through the system based on the historical probability of transitioning from one state to another (for example, the probability of being promoted or the probability of leaving).[1] Push models often

---

[1] The terms "push model" and "Markov model" are often used interchangeably in the workforce planning literature. However, we note that a Markov model implies that a model

assume that worker flows will be equal to historical flow rates and estimate changes in the stocks of workers given these flows. A simple push model generally starts with the stock of workers in period t, adds the expected number of gains, and subtracts the predicted number of losses to arrive at the predicted stock of workers in period $t+1$. The gains and losses are often analyzed on an annual basis, although organizations with high turnover may forecast on a quarterly basis instead.

Using push flows is appropriate when transitions are not dependent on the availability of positions. For example, the Bureau of Health Professions' physician supply model uses a stock-and-flow concept in which the population of doctors is naturally aged every year (U.S. Department of Health and Human Services, 2008). Similarly, the RAND Inventory Model contains both push and pull characteristics; a key push characteristic is that it automatically moves each cohort of workers to the next year of service (Gates et al., 2008). These natural aging processes are suited to push modeling.

Box 3.1: The RAND Inventory Model

The RAND Inventory Model is a stock-and-flow supply projection model that uses Defense Civilian Personnel Data System (DCPDS) data. The model calculates average separation, new-hire, switch-in, and switch-out rates for the previous five years. Separations are individuals who leave the DoD workforce, while new hires are employees who were previously not in DoD. Switches in are employees who were previously in another part of the civilian DoD workforce but have moved into the subpopulation of interest. Similarly, switches out are employees who move out of the subpopulation of interest but remain in the civilian DoD organization. The period of five years is used because it strikes a balance between long-run and short-run trends. On one hand, if a shorter horizon, say one year of historical data, were used and the data for that year were unusual, the abnormality would percolate through the model's projections. Using a five-year

---

is "memoryless"; that is, future changes depend only on the information contained in the current state. Therefore, it is possible to have a "push" model that is not a Markov model, in the sense that future changes depend on past history.

Box 3.1—continued

horizon smooths such abnormal effects. On the other hand, if a longer horizon—say ten or 20 years—were used, the data would include a time when the workforce looked significantly different than it does today. Using a five-year horizon sidesteps this potential problem and is likely to seem reasonable from a manager's point of view.

Historical separation and switch-out rates are calculated separately by years relative to retirement eligibility (YORE): The number of separations or switches out is divided by the baseline population in that YORE. Historical new-hire rates are calculated by using the overall new-hire rate (new hires divided by baseline population). In using these rates to project the total number of new hires, the model assumes that new hires are distributed across YORE as they were historically. Switch-in rates are calculated similarly.

The starting point for the projection is the number of DoD employees in year t, by YORE. The following steps are taken:

- The employees in YORE X are "aged" by one year, to move to YORE $X+1$.
- The separation rate for employees in YORE X is multiplied by the number of employees in that YORE to project the number of employees in YORE X who leave DoD from the subpopulation of interest.
- The switch-out rate for employees in YORE X is multiplied by the number of employees in that YORE to project the number of employees in YORE X who remain in DoD but leave the subpopulation of interest.
- The overall new-hire rate, coupled with the distribution of those new hires in YORE $X+1$, is used to project the number of employees who join DoD in the subpopulation of interest.
- The overall switch-in rate, coupled with the distribution of those switches into YORE $X+1$, is used to project the number of employees who move from another part of DoD into the subpopulation of interest.

Box 3.1—continued

- The size of the workforce in YORE $X+1$, in year $t+1$, is estimated by taking the population from YORE X, subtracting separations and switches out, and adding new hires and switches in.

This procedure is applied to each YORE category and to each subsequent year. Separation rates differ by retirement plan, and new employees are typically hired under the Federal Employees Retirement System (FERS) retirement plan. Therefore, the model separately projects an inventory of employees in the FERS plan, the Civil Service Retirement System (CSRS) plan, and other retirement plans and then adds these estimates to generate an overall projection.

There are two basic versions of the model. Both versions of the model project historical separation, switch-in, and switch-out rates into the future. The first version also projects historical new-hire rates into the future. In the second version, the user specifies the desired end strength in each year, and the model calculates the new-hire rate necessary to achieve the desired end strengths. In both versions, if the user believes that historical separation or switching rates will not hold in the future, he or she can enter alternative rates. In the first version of the model, the user can also specify alternative new-hire rates.

The RAND Inventory Model has been used in a variety of applications. It was originally developed to support supply projections for the acquisition workforce (Emmerichs, Marcum, and Robbert, 2004) and has been used to project the supply of the acquisition workforce under various hiring scenarios (Gates et al., 2008). Currently, the model is used to provide ongoing projections of workforce supply for the acquisition workforce and for a number of mission-critical occupations within DoD, including estimates of the number of new hires (or forced separations) required to meet target workforce levels.

A key decision in a push model is how to estimate flow, or transition, rates. Voluntary separation rates are particularly challenging, as organizations typically have less control over separation than they do over hiring or promotion. Projected rates are typically based on historical rates in some way.

Planners can project future rates based on *cohort analysis,* which follows a group of similar employees over time and extrapolates past behavior into the future for that group of individuals. Alternatively, they can use *census analysis*, which projects future rates based on several cohorts (Edwards, 1983).

Planners also have several choices with respect to how to extrapolate historical rates into the future. For example, the Civilian Forecasting System (CIVFORS) allows users to select between taking a simple average of historical rates and assuming that these rates hold in the future, taking weighted averages of historical rates with more recent years receiving higher weights, and projecting out trends in historical rates into the future.

Rates may be calculated separately for different groups of workers. The Bureau of Health Professions' physician supply model estimates historical attrition rates and projects them into the future, separately for each age and gender group. Supply projections are performed separately for each medical specialty (U.S. Department of Health and Human Services, 2008).

Box 3.2: Integrated Workforce Analysis and Planning Model

Another workforce supply tool currently used within DoD is the Defense Logistics Agency's (DLA's) Integrated Workforce Analysis and Planning Model (IWAPM), developed by Serco Inc. IWAPM can be used to forecast supply by occupation, Primary Level Field Activities (PLFA), and grade level.

According to our discussions with Serco representatives, the model uses an algorithm to identify historical trends in separation rates and to project those rates into the future. The rates can be calculated separately for various groups (for example, by occupation or age). This model draws on DCPDS data; the data are updated quarterly as new DCPDS data become available, and the new data are

---

Box 3.2—continued

incorporated into historical rate calculations. IWAPM has an online interface, so managers can access the tool themselves.

The supply projections can be compared to user-specified targets. Users can assume steady-state demand (the number of employees stays fixed), assume zero-target demand (to examine only separation patterns), or enter customized targets. The tool will then display the gap between demand and projected supply.

Serco representatives suggested two caveats when conducting forecasts at disaggregated levels. First, users must be cautious about interpreting the data for small groups of employees; Serco cautions users that the results are not "statistically significant" for these small populations. Second, users must be aware of how the DCPDS data are structured; for example, interns in DLA are all assigned to the central level, regardless of where they are located, and therefore do not show up in different PLFAs. These caveats are common to all stock-and-flow models that use DCPDS data.

The second main category of stock-and-flow models is a pull model. A pull model (also known as a *renewal* model) moves workers into the organization, or into certain positions, based on whether positions are available. Unlike a push model, which uses estimated worker flows to project future worker stocks, a pull model takes as given the demand for the number of workers in each position, as well as the separation rates associated with each position, and estimates the hiring and promotion flows needed to fill those positions.

Pull models typically develop "rules" or "fill rates" that specify how vacant positions should be filled. The model first projects the number of vacancies in the most senior level that are expected due to separations or expansion of demand. The rules specify what fraction of the vacancies should be filled by promotions from various internal employee groups or from new hires. Promotions from lower levels create additional vacancies in those levels. The model then works its way down organizational levels using similar rules about how to fill vacancies created by promotions, separations, or expanded demand at each level (Bechet and Maki, 1987).

Pull models are typically used in situations where there is control over employee movement and where the required numbers of workers in particular positions are known. Basic pull models assume that vacancies are instantaneously filled, but more sophisticated models can incorporate delays for filling positions. The advantage of incorporating delays is that managers can model the expected number of vacancies at any level in the organization at a given time (Bartholomew and Forbes, 1979).

In practice, both push and pull factors play a role in workforce management, and many models combine both types of elements or allow users to choose the element that suits their situation. For example, in the RAND Military Career Model, users can choose to assume that a certain percentage of people from each grade are promoted each year (a push factor) or that people are only promoted when vacancies are available in a higher grade (a pull factor).

There are several advantages of using stock-and-flow models for supply projections. First, stock-and-flow models rely on historical transition rates, which can often be easily calculated based on available human resources data. Second, a stock-and-flow model can be made fairly transparent to users so that they can understand what drives model outcomes. Third, a stock-and-flow model (particularly a push model) can mimic the natural aging process of the workforce, whether through actual aging (as for the physician workforce) or through aging in terms of years of service.

There are, however, a number of limitations to stock-and-flow models. These models project future trends and allow users to ask what would happen under different sets of assumptions, but they do not identify the optimal way to achieve a particular goal, such as minimizing cost. They also require sample sizes on the order of hundreds of workers, as transition rates calculated based on smaller population sizes may be unstable (Wang, 2005).

Stock-and-flow models also require the selection of an appropriate historical period for calculating flow rates. Often, the past few years of data are used. Alternatively, if a planner thinks that a prior period will more closely approximate future trends, data from that period may be used to project rates. Selecting the appropriate historical period is challenging, since worker flows in every period will be influenced by a variety of factors, including organizational policies and economic conditions.

Another limitation is their deterministic nature—that is, they only produce one number, rather than a confidence interval. Thus, small changes in transaction rates can yield large differences in projected supply. The accuracy of these models may deteriorate as the time horizon lengthens (O'Brien-Pallas et al., 2001).

One way to address the concern about the deterministic nature of the stock-and-flow model is to provide a range of estimates, rather than one number (Lomas, Stoddart, and Barer, 1985). Many studies conduct sensitivity analyses, varying assumptions about future transition rates or other key factors, particularly those that are more uncertain. For example, the physician supply model discussed above complements its supply estimates by showing how supply would change under various assumptions about physician productivity, retirement rates, and medical school graduation rates. As we would expect, the projected ranges increase in later years, as small differences are compounded over time (U.S. Department of Health and Human Services, 2008).

A few authors have incorporated stochastic elements into stock-and-flow models. For example, Joyce, McNeil, and Stoelwinder (2006) forecast the supply of physicians in Australia using a stock-and-flow model. Instead of simply using point estimates for key input values, they take a Latin Hypercube Sample over a range of plausible input values and conduct a Monte Carlo simulation based on the sampled input parameters. This allows them to construct confidence intervals around the projected supply estimates.

The concern that model accuracy degrades over time also suggests that the models should be frequently updated, as new information about historical rates becomes available. Such updates can be part of Step 5 of the workforce planning process described in Chapter One, which involves monitoring and updating progress toward closing gaps in supply and demand.

Box 3.3: Intelligence Community Workforce Models

Trice, Bertelli, and Ward (2011) describe a set of workforce planning tools that were developed for the Intelligence Community. The Intelligence Community grew quickly after the September 11, 2001, attacks, but this growth has proved unsustainable, given pending budget cuts, and has led to an increased interest in strategic workforce planning. The study conducted cost analyses for different potential workforce scenarios based on demographics, retention policies and practices, the government/industry mix, and associated infrastructure costs. In addition to a basic model, which is similar to the stock-and-flow models described above, these tools include models for analyzing the civilian/contractor mix and for examining the potential cost savings from lowering grades associated with positions.

- The Workforce Demographics Model is a traditional Markov model that projects the size of the civilian workforce by grade over a six-year timeframe. The model measures turnover by years to optional retirement, which is broken into six bands by the number of years each individual has until retirement age. The number of hires is set equal to attrition plus desired workforce growth. This type of broad planning is crucial to ensure that the Intelligence Community has the right workforce to achieve its core objectives.
- The Workforce Mix Model helps determine the optimal mix of civilian and contractor employees needed to minimize costs. Although contractors tend to be more expensive, they are more flexible and more cost-efficient for short-term projects. Contractors may also provide expertise in areas where civilian employees are lacking. The model examines the implications of changing the total force and mix of contractor and civilian forces over a five-year period. The overall costs for different force mixes are calculated as a function of the average costs for civilians and contractors. The model is also used to create scenarios by which civilians can replace contractor personnel at different growth rates.

Box 3.3—continued

- The Regrading Model estimates the cost savings of lowering the grades of 10 percent of positions each year for a five-year period. Positions are only regraded once they become vacant due to turnover. Gradually lowering the average grade of the civilian workforce over time is one way for the Intelligence Community to cut manpower costs. However, intelligence workers are not highly paid to begin with, so the authors note that lowering salaries further may lead to a significant amount of skill loss.

Systems Dynamics Models

Systems dynamics models are similar to stock-and-flow models, but they incorporate feedback loops and allow potential time delays between inputs and output. Kirkwood (2013) describes feedback as "the phenomenon where changes in the values of a variable indirectly influence future values of that same variable" (p. 29). A simple example of a systems dynamics model is presented by Wang (2007). It is based on a stock-and-flow model: All recruiting occurs at the most junior level, and officers who successfully complete training progress up the ranks. The key feature that differentiates this model from a standard stock-and-flow model is that it is a *closed loop* system. Recruiting affects the number of trainees, which affects the number of officers, which in turn affects recruiting decisions.

Systems dynamics models have reportedly been used for human resources planning within DoD in various instances. Systems dynamics models have been developed for Army planning involving enlisted personnel and pilots, as well as for certain Navy workforce planning exercises (Wang, 2005). Several government agencies in Australia, including the Tax Office, the Army, and the Navy, also use systems dynamics models (Linard, 2003).

A key advantage of a systems dynamics model is that it explicitly models the potential feedback from one part of a system to another. A simple stock-and-flow model may assume that retention rates are fixed based on historical averages or may allow users to manually change retention rates. In contrast, a systems dynamics model may recognize that conditions within the system, such as a change in the availability of vacant positions (and thus promotion opportunities), may also affect retention rates; the model can explicitly account for the potential impact of such changes. However, compared with stock-and-flow models, systems dynamics models are more difficult to develop and less transparent to users. In addition, systems dynamics models are often solved by computer simulation rather than analytically. As a result, the availability of computing resources and the time required to solve the model will factor into whether a systems dynamics model is appropriate for a particular application.

Regression Models

Regression methods explicitly recognize that there are unanticipated factors that affect outcomes of interest and introduce "noise" or "disturbances" to account for such factors.[2] Two broad types of regression techniques can be used: time-series methods and cross-sectional methods. A simple time-series method may forecast the future value of an outcome of interest based on past values of that outcome, as well as on past values of random disturbances. Such a model is known as an autoregressive moving average (ARMA) model (Greene, 2003). The nature of the disturbance term that is assumed and the number of previous values used in the forecast are modeling choices.

Cross-sectional methods model an outcome of interest as a function of other variables observed at the same time, as well as a random disturbance term. As with time-series models, the specific variables included and the assumptions made about the disturbance term are modeling choices. Panel data methods combine both time-series and cross-sectional approaches.

---

[2] As discussed above, stochastic elements can also be incorporated into stock-and-flow models.

There are few examples of purely regression-based models on the supply side.[3] One example involves the Bureau of Labor Statistics' (BLS's) projections for future U.S. employment levels. BLS begins with the U.S. Census Bureau's projections of the civilian noninstitutional population. Labor force participation rates are then projected for each of 136 groups by age, gender, and ethnicity, using time-series extrapolation methods. The total labor force is estimated by multiplying the projected participation rate for each group by the projected population in each group. This supply (labor force) projection is then used as an input to a macroeconomic model of the economy to produce employment estimates by industry and occupation, assuming full employment (Sommers and Franklin, 2012).

More commonly, regression methods are used to improve forecasts of transition rates. For example, Pinfield (1981) presents a case study of an organization that faced extremely high termination rates at one of its plants. Managers developed an exponential smoothing model to forecast terminations based on past history.

The transition rates projected by regression models can also be integrated with stock-and-flow techniques. For example, time-series methods may be used to extrapolate historical workforce transition rates into the future, and those rates can be used in stock-and-flow models in lieu of historical averages. In addition, cross-sectional methods may be used to relate workforce characteristics to separation rates so that projected separation rates can be adjusted to accommodate anticipated changes in workforce composition.

One example of a stock-and-flow model that incorporates regression techniques is CIVFORS. CIVFORS uses a Poisson regression model to estimate the number of separations and gains based on such user-selected variables as years of service and pay grade. In addition, users may select from a variety of methods, including regression techniques, for projecting historical trends into the future. These projected separation and gain rates are then incorporated into a stock-and-flow model.

---

[3] In contrast, both time-series and cross-sectional methods are used on the demand side. These techniques are discussed in more detail in the following chapter.

Another example can be found in Angus et al. (2000), who use a stock-and-flow technique to predict the number of physicians. To predict the number of hours worked by each physician, they use a cross-sectional regression model to estimate the relationship between hours worked and various characteristics, including physician age, gender, specialty, faculty status, and degree of managed care penetration into the local market. The regression model allows them to project future hours worked based on an expected set of future workforce characteristics (for example, a different age profile). Total physician supply is then estimated as the number of physicians multiplied by hours worked by each physician.

One key advantage of using a regression model is that it explicitly accounts for uncertainty associated with the outcomes of interest, thus producing not only one number, but a likely range, for future estimates. It also provides planners with a variety of methods for projecting historical trends into the future, and for estimating the effects of changing workforce characteristics on supply.

Regression models have a number of drawbacks as well. First, results may change substantially when different modeling choices (for example, assumptions about the disturbance term, included variables, or form of the regression) are used; the appropriate modeling choices will vary based on the situation and may not always be clear. Second, like stock-and-flow models, regression models rely on projecting past information into the future and thus require judgment when applied to organizations that are changing rapidly. Third, like stock-and-flow models, regression models do not help a user to determine the optimal way to achieve a goal, such as minimizing cost.

Box 3.4: Civilian Forecasting System

Like the RAND Inventory Model, CIVFORS is a stock-and-flow model that draws on DCPDS data. CIVFORS was developed based on an Army forecasting tool and uses data from the previous five years to project gain rates (including new hires, switches into the subpopulation of interest, and movements from inactive to active status) as well as loss rates (separations, switches out, and employees moving from active to inactive status). "Migrations"

Box 3.4—continued

within the subpopulation of interest, such as changes in occupational series or grade levels, are also considered (U.S. Army, Civilian Human Resources Agency, Assistant G-1 for Civilian Personnel, 2006).

CIVFORS models each historical rate as a function of user-selected worker characteristics (called "predictive data elements"). A Poisson regression model, which estimates the relationship between the number of transactions (for example, the number of accessions) and worker characteristics (for example, years of service and gender), is part of the methodology for generating historical rates. CIVFORS offers a variety of data-mining algorithms to help users select an appropriate set of variables for predicting transaction rates. Users can also specify "proportionally distributed data elements" that project historical proportions into the future. For example, suppose that gender is selected as a proportionally distributed data element: If 30 percent of the workforce is female, then 30 percent of the forecasted information will be for females (U.S. Office of Personnel Management, 2003).

Users may select from among several methods for projecting historical rates into the future. These methods include calculating a weighted average of historical data (based on a default system that weights recent years more heavily or based on user-specified weights) and projecting a historical trend into the future. Other optional features account for seasonality in rates and provide various methods for dealing with outliers. Small cell size issues are addressed by using a "hierarchical procedure that seeks to produce rates based on sufficient data" (U.S. Office of Personnel Management, 2003).

Users may choose a model that projects historical rates into the future or one that attempts to meet target strengths. For example, when applied to Army personnel, targets are based on the Army's Structure and Manpower Allocation System (SAMAS), which provides authorized and budgeted positions. SAMAS authorizations are typically available by major Army

Box 3.4—continued

command and unit identification code (UIC). Therefore, if the user conducts the analysis at a different level, the authorizations are proportionally assigned across groups. Alternatively, users can choose a "steady-state" option that maintains the current size of the workforce. The default option is to meet targets by changing new-hire rates (U.S. Army, Civilian Human Resources Agency, Assistant G-1 for Civilian Personnel, 2006).

CIVFORS offers a considerable amount of flexibility. Options include

- selecting the number of historical quarters to use in estimating rates
- selecting the number of quarters for projections
- selecting the level of drill-down (such as occupation, pay grade, or subcommand)
- selecting variables that are used in estimating historical rates and in applying historical factors to projected strengths (predictive and proportionally distributed data elements, as discussed above)
- creating a new grouping for an existing variable (for example, creating age groups using the age variable)
- selecting a method for projecting historical rates into the future (discussed above) or manually changing rates
- forecasting specific types of transaction rates (for example, forecasting transactions by Nature of Action code)
- selecting targets for the aggregate population or for subsets of the population (for example, by pay grade)
- selecting alternative ways of meeting targets (for example, changing separations or, if targets are by pay grade, changing promotions)
- establishing constraints on end strengths or on transaction rates.

Optimization Models

Whereas stock-and-flow, systems dynamics, and regression models are predictive in nature because they project future labor supply based on historical trends, optimization models are goal-oriented. These models identify policies that optimize certain metrics given a set of constraints, such as future manpower requirements. They are useful for a workforce planner who knows how many personnel he or she wants in the future but is unsure of how he or she should hire and promote to meet that objective. They can also be useful for a workforce planner who wants to meet a specific and quantifiable goal, such as minimizing cost.

The goals that the planner seeks to achieve and the requirements that the planner faces are modeled with *objective functions* and *constraints,* respectively. Optimization models find solutions that maximize or minimize the objective functions subject to the user-specified constraints. The objective functions and constraints together form the mathematical program, a mathematical expression of the problem facing a workforce planner. A mathematical program may have only one objective function—for example, to minimize cost—or may have multiple objective functions—for example, to minimize cost and to maximize readiness. Setting up a mathematical program requires selecting and parameterizing mathematical expressions capturing objective functions and constraints. It is often not a trivial task to even decide what is an objective and what is a constraint. For example, a workforce planner may wish to minimize cost subject to a few known constraints on readiness or may wish to minimize cost and maximize some metric related to readiness. The two approaches will yield different mathematical programs to solve within an optimization model.

Linear programming is sometimes used in workforce planning. Linear programming is used to solve mathematical programs with a single objective function and several constraints, all of which involve linear functions of *decision variables*. Decision variables model the choices and actions of the workforce planner/decisionmaker. In the case of linear programming, decision variables are continuous variables. Integer programming involves using decision variables that are required to be integers. Mixed integer linear programming involves mathematical programs where some decision variables are integers and some are continuous in the context of an objective function and several constraints that are linear in the decision variables. Suppose a planner knows the manpower requirements for several job categories. His or her objective is to minimize the costs of recruitment, training, transfers, and redundancies. He or she must meet this objective subject to the constraints of (1) achieving the manpower requirements and (2) allowing for the expected flows of workers between various classes within the organization (for example, grades). He or she therefore attempts to identify the numbers of recruits and redundancies (assuming these are under his or her control) that would minimize cost subject to the constraints (Wang, 2005). This would likely involve an application of mixed integer linear programming, one form of mathematical programming. If decision variables reflecting recruit and redundancy numbers were allowed to be continuous variables, linear programming could be used.

There are often multiple, competing criteria to consider. For example, an organization may want to target end strength along with promotion and hiring rates (Gass, 1986). The field of multi-criteria decisionmaking extends mathematical programming concepts and techniques to consider such situations. Goal programming is one area within the field of multi-criteria decisionmaking that seeks to select goal values for several criteria and then to find a feasible management policy that performs well, relative to the goal value, for each criteria (Niehaus, 1980). In goal programming, each of the criteria is expressed as an elastic constraint, a constraint where the criteria goal is set equal to the result of the management policy under consideration plus some "slack" captured via an artificial decision variable. The math program seeks to minimize a weighted sum of the slack variables, or, in other words, a weighted sum of the deviations from all goals. Planners can assign priorities to each goal so that the programming technique places more emphasis on meeting the higher priority goals. A downside to this system is that it can force the user to manually weight many goals; this is a nontrivial task and may not be feasible in some situations. Another disadvantage of goal programming is that small changes in how criteria are weighted can cause large changes to the solution (Silverman, Steuer, and Whisman, 1988).[4]

Feuer (1983) provides a simple example of a goal programming exercise. In his example, a university planner seeks to meet five objectives (expressed as constraints), including a maximum wage bill as a fraction of tuition revenue, a maximum rise in tuition over time, a minimum fluctuation in the rate of faculty advancement, a maximum ratio of tenured to nontenured faculty, and a maximum ratio of full professors to assistant professors. The goal of the exercise is to minimize deviations from these objectives. The planner ranks each of the objectives and specifies the relative importance of each one, as well as whether he or she prefers deviations above or below the objectives (for example, he or she may prefer to come in slightly under rather than over budget). These priorities are incorporated into the objective function. The model then identifies internal advancement rates, tuition rates, and new hires that meet the prioritized goals as closely as possible.

Optimization models are not frequently used for manpower planning. Few manpower planners have training in optimization techniques, and established mathematical programs for workforce planning are rare. However, we describe a few relevant prior efforts below.

An example of a linear programming model is the Accession Supply Costing and Requirements (ASCAR) Model. ASCAR was built for the Congressional Budget Office and the Office of the Assistant Secretary of Defense to evaluate their enlisted personnel levels during the 1970s and 1980s (Collins, Gass, and Rosendahl, 1983). ASCAR can optimize for end strength, trained end strength, and total man-years, while setting constraints on the characteristics of new recruits across such variables as race, education level, and scores on mental aptitude tests. Different combinations of these variables are used to define 60 supply categories of personnel based on demographics. A linear program calculates how many recruits should come from each demo-

---

[4] The Tchebycheff procedure corrects some of the problems that characterize traditional goal programming by automatically generating weights and by displaying multiple solutions for different trade-offs (Silverman, Steuer, and Whisman, 1988).

graphic group, while minimizing the deviations from the set goals, to achieve the optimal force mix.

The Enlisted Loss Inventory Model—Computation of Manpower Programs Using Linear Programming (ELIM-COMPLIP) was a system used by the Army to determine the number of personnel to recruit or draft to maintain a set force level during the 1970s (Holz and Wroth, 1980). COMPLIP was a linear program designed to minimize the absolute weighted sum of the deviations from the target strength. Previously, the Army had overrecruited to hedge against the uncertainty of future manpower levels. COMPLIP was credited for saving $100 million by improving the accuracy of forecasts and decreasing the need to overrecruit.

Manganaris (2013) documents the use of a linear program to match "faces" with "spaces" during a restructuring of the Internal Revenue Service. He notes that the objective was to minimize the "cost" of matches. An exact match between an available person and an available space (for example, in terms of pay grade and location) was assigned a small cost, with higher costs associated with poorer matches. The resulting model allowed the identification of "misalignments" between personnel and positions. In addition, misalignment in mission-critical occupations was used as a feedback mechanism to adjust the planned structure of the workforce.

Several academic papers have also presented optimization models for forecasting military manpower supply. Gass (1986) proposes a manpower model that forecasts movement between seven grades over a 20-year period by assigning weights to policy goals, such as end strength, promotion rate, and loss rate. The technique is novel in that the algorithm automatically assigns weights, rather than forcing the user to do so manually. A more recent example is the Requirements-Driven Cost-Based Optimization (RCMOP) Model, a linear program that recommends naval officer promotions and accessions to meet budget constraints (Clark, 2009). The program works by minimizing an objective function of a penalty associated with not meeting personnel requirements.

Simulation Techniques

Simple models can be solved analytically, using mathematical methods. More complex models may not have an analytic solution (or may be difficult to solve analytically). In this case, the relationships that constitute the model may be simulated using a computer.

Although simulation models are often considered a separate category of manpower models, simulation methods can be applied to any type of model. For example, the systems dynamics model discussed above (Wang, 2007) includes complex feedback loops that do not easily admit an analytic solution; rather, the author uses simulation techniques to examine the effects of various policy changes on the number of officers.

A key benefit of using simulation techniques is that they allow more complex behaviors and relationships. All models require that real-world relationships be simplified in order to admit analysis and solution, but the problem can be particularly acute with analytic models that require closed-form relationships among parameters of interest (O'Brien-Pallas et al., 2001). Simulation models may be particularly useful when complex individual behavior is modeled. For example, RAND has developed a dynamic retention model that analyzes the stay-leave decisions made by individual military members; this model assumes that individuals maximize their utility by comparing future income streams from military versus civilian positions. Stochastic elements are incorporated by assuming random shocks in each year. After estimating the parameters of the model, the model simulates the behavior of individuals under alternative policy regimes (Mattock, Hosek, and Asch, 2012).

The incorporation of stochastic elements in the model cited above is aided by the choice of using simulation rather than analytic techniques (Edwards, 1983). Simulation techniques may also be more appropriate for modeling small employee populations, as analytic models are often based on assumed equilibrium, long-run, or large-population-size conditions. However, applying simulation techniques to large groups of employees may require more computational power and time than an organization has available. As computational availability increases, this limitation is less likely to be a challenge. Other drawbacks of simulation modeling include the need for detailed data (Edwards, 1983) and the fact that users who are not familiar with simulation techniques may find it challenging to run such models.

Box 3.5: RAND Military Career Model

The RAND Military Career Model (MCM) is an example of a stock-and-flow model that uses simulation techniques and incorporates a number of stochastic elements. This model uses both push and pull factors to assign, promote, and retire simulated military officers according to user-defined rules. The rules can be changed to reflect policy changes and to examine how such changes would affect overall outcomes, such as end strengths, as well as the career patterns of officers.

Users can choose to run MCM for various populations, including occupation groups or entire services. The user must specify a number of inputs, or rules, that the model will follow, including:

- number of authorizations
- how accessions are made
- how retention is modeled
- job requirements
- various rules for promotions, including maximum allowable time-in-grade, promotion mechanism, and mandatory time-in-grade after promotion.

Users can select from among a number of accession models, including hiring a fixed number of individuals into each grade during each period or hiring individuals to fill vacancies. MCM can also handle a variety of retention models. A simple option is for users to specify retention rates by grade and year. The appropriate separation rate is then applied to each individual stochastically. For example, if the separation probability for individuals in grade 6 is 20 percent, then the model essentially rolls a weighted die for each individual in grade 6, so that each individual has a 20-percent chance of leaving. MCM can also incorporate separation rates generated by a dynamic retention model (discussed briefly earlier in this chapter; see Mattock, Hosek, and Asch, 2012 for more details).

Box 3.5—continued

Promotions may be driven by push or pull factors. Users can choose "opportunity-driven" promotions (an example of a push factor), which promote a certain percentage of people from each grade. Alternatively, users can choose "vacancy-driven promotions" (an example of a pull factor), which promote people to meet the number of authorizations in each grade.

MCM also has a "jobs" module, which allows users to specify jobs to be filled. Jobs can have both positive requirements (required or desired specialties) and negative requirements (undesirable specialties). The model then selects individuals who best meet the job requirements. If more than one individual is equally qualified for a vacant job, the model can randomly select among them. Alternatively, each individual is assigned an "aptitude" score (a randomly assigned number drawn from a normal distribution), which can be used as a tiebreaker for job assignments.

MCM has been used extensively in published and unpublished RAND work, including analyzing the effects of lengthening assignments and careers for active-duty officers (Schirmer et al., 2006) and evaluating the feasibility of managing the end-strength accounting rules required by the National Defense Authorization Act Fiscal Year 2009 (Schirmer, 2009).

Replacement Charts and Succession Planning

Replacement charts involve identifying potential vacancies in higher-level positions, as well as strategies for filling those vacancies with lower-level employees. In the longer term, organizations often use succession planning to identify employees who can fill critical positions. Potential candidates can be identified based on their skills and competencies, and their careers developed to prepare them for future leadership roles. The planning exercise can also serve to highlight skill gaps within the organization (Bulmash, Chhinzer, and Speers, 2010). These gaps can alert managers to the potential need for training of current employees, or external hiring, to fill critical positions.

Unlike the methods described above, replacement charts and succession planning identify specific individuals who are currently in the organization and could be promoted or trained. These tools would typically be used to ensure smooth transitions for senior-level positions rather than for overall workforce planning. For example, NASA recognizes the need for succession planning for key positions under its operational (short-term) planning process (NASA, 2008).

Box 3.6: Other Tools

We spoke with several vendors who create proprietary workforce planning tools for private and government organizations about their tools. In this section, we provide a brief summary of the tools provided by two vendors.

Human Capital Management Institute has a Workforce Planning Tool, which we were told is based on a stock-and-flow model. The tool can be set up to allow users to examine specific groups of employees (for example, by job group or role). The tool can also be used to model workforce demand based on organizational drivers, such as budget, and to examine gaps between demand and supply.

We also spoke with SAS regarding their workforce analytics tools. One of their tools uses time-series regression techniques to forecast future workforce supply. The tool creates forecasts using approximately three dozen models and selects the model with the best statistical fit. Forecasts can be performed at various levels of disaggregation, and the tool reconciles disaggregated results with the aggregate forecast. The model can optimize workforce supply given user-specific constraints on budget or schedule. SAS representatives indicated that they typically create demand models for commercial firms, using sales projections to forecast workforce demand.

Other Considerations

External Supply Analysis

Most of the models above focus on "internal supply" forecasting; they model flows of current employees and assume that new-hire rates will either continue as in the past or be manipulated to meet future requirements. However, it may also be important to consider the "external supply"—how feasible it will be to find new employees with required competencies.

Few supply projection models have explicitly considered external labor supply when forecasting new hires.[5] Rather, external supply analyses are typically used to identify specific competencies that may be difficult to find and thus to inform the gap analysis and implementation plan (Steps 3 and 4 in the workforce planning process outlined in Chapter One). One example of external labor supply analysis is the Available Labor Force (AVAIL) Model, which was created for the Navy in the context of equal opportunity employment planning. The AVAIL model uses census data for local labor markets (metropolitan areas or regions), along with information about wages, to project trends in the availability of workers. For example, the model can be used to analyze the effect of changing Navy wages on "attracted pools" of workers or the effect of changing Navy wages relative to private sector wages on the desirability of Navy jobs (Niehaus, 1988; Atwater, Nelson, and Niehaus, 1991).

Data on current external supply may come from such sources as the Bureau of Labor Statistics or state-level labor departments, which collect employment and wage data by occupation. Data on future external supply could be based on estimates of the number of graduates in various fields from a variety of sources, such as the U.S. Census, the U.S. Department of Education, local educational institutions, or private organizations, such as the National Student Clearinghouse. Local,

---

[5] In contrast, many military manpower studies have taken external conditions into account when examining projected separation rates. These studies typically examine stay-leave decisions of enlisted members and officers by comparing opportunities and wages within the military with those in the private sector. For a review of such retention models, see Asch, Hosek, and Warner (2007).

rather than national, data on the potential pool of external workers can be helpful, particularly in remote areas, as workers may not be willing to relocate (Australian Public Service Commission, 2011).

Masi et al. (2009) conducted an external supply analysis for the Army HRC during its relocation to Fort Knox, near Louisville, as part of the 2005 Base Closure and Realignment Commission (BRAC) legislation. Since many existing employees might not have been willing to relocate to Fort Knox, the authors identified several potential groups of employees that HRC could draw upon: other civil service personnel in Fort Knox whose departments were moving out of Fort Knox because of BRAC; the local workforce in the Fort Knox area; the national workforce; military retirees, inactive reservists, and military spouses; and future generations of workers in the area. For each potential worker pool, the authors evaluated the likelihood that those workers would be willing to work at HRC and considered whether they would provide a good match in terms of competencies. For example, the authors compared the average wages earned by human resource and information technology workers (two types of workers likely to be needed) in the Louisville area with typical General Schedule salaries to gauge the potential for attracting workers to HRC. Their analysis of external supply, although based on some quantitative data for each worker pool, is largely qualitative.

Summary

Before turning to the demand side, we note that supply projections are almost always based on projecting historical workforce patterns into the future. This may be a reasonable assumption when an organization is experiencing a relatively stable period, but is unlikely to be true during times of major change. In addition, historical stocks and flows of workers represent *equilibrium* outcomes—a combination of both supply and demand factors. Historical separation rates reflect the willingness of current workers to continue working (supply), which is in turn influenced by a variety of factors that are internal to the organization (for example, how current management is viewed by employees), as well as external factors (for example, the unemployment rate). Separation rates may also reflect early retirement incentive packages offered by the company because of reduced staffing needs (demand).

Historical trends can be useful in providing a baseline forecast. However, managers should not assume that these forecasts would necessarily be accurate in the future, particularly during times of change. In addition, historical data reflect equilibria driven by a combination of supply and demand conditions. As a result, managers should incorporate judgment about expected future changes into their planning. Many of the tools we have discussed throughout this chapter allow the user to change historical rates to reflect projected changes in both supply factors (for example, reduced availability of certain types of workers) and demand factors (for example, a hiring freeze).

CHAPTER FOUR

Demand Models: Issues and Options

Determining workforce demand involves identifying the total number of workers, the type of workers (military, civilian, or contractor), and the job competencies needed to maintain an organization's missions and goals. Demand often can be more difficult to forecast than supply because of the sheer number of environmental and organizational factors that influence demand. Consequently, a number of quantitative and qualitative techniques are available to forecast workforce demand, and in practice, the decision of which technique to employ will depend on the size, expertise, and resources available to the organization.

This chapter focuses on reviewing techniques used by both the private and public sectors to assess workforce demand. We begin by describing the basic steps and components common across all techniques. Then we describe different ways to project future demand. These range from quantitative techniques, which mathematically model the relationship between demand drivers and the required workforce, to qualitative techniques, which are able to inform not only the appropriate size but also the ideal composition and competencies of the workforce. In addition, we review techniques that combine quantitative and qualitative aspects, using both top-down and bottom-up approaches. Along the way, we highlight the advantages and disadvantages of each technique in terms of feasibility and usefulness.

Before turning to the details of workforce demand planning, let us clarify a semantic distinction between workforce requirements and workforce authorizations that is rooted in the legislative guidance governing DoD's management of its civilian workforce. The terms "requirements" and "authorizations" are often used interchangeably to refer to workforce demand, but requirements and authorizations should not be considered equivalent. Under 10 U.S.C. 129, "The civilian personnel of the Department of Defense shall be managed each fiscal year solely on the basis of and consistent with (1) the workload required to carry out the functions and activities of the department and (2) the funds made available to the department for such fiscal year " (p. 108). The first consideration defines the workforce requirements; the second determines the number of authorizations. It is the combination of requirements and authorizations that will affect what workforce size can actually be achieved. Gates et al. (2006) note that in DoD, organizations are staffed to authorizations, rather than requirements, and this additional constraint complicates workforce planning within DoD. Therefore, it is important to recognize that workforce requirements will differ from, and often be higher than, workforce authorizations.

Basic Components and Steps of Workforce Demand Analysis

Regardless of the technique, there are three basic steps in projecting future workforce demand. First, an organization will assess current workforce demand by considering three components:

1. total workload
2. individual worker productivity
3. total workforce size.

This information is used to examine the relationship between workload and required workforce. In a simplified way, dividing the total work to be done by some measure of worker productivity generates an estimate of the current number of workers needed by the organization to accomplish the work. Measures of current total workload are often based on the desired outcomes of business units—e.g., the number of airplanes to be acquired, bombs to be produced, or engines to be upgraded (Vernez et al., 2007). Measures of productivity differ across occupations and organizations; for example, purchasing and contracting organizations use key performance indexes, such as average time to complete an action, average dollar volume obligated per buyer, and mean cost per dollar obligated.[1] Reed (2011) reviews the academic literature and notes that, ideally, productivity measures should also account for the type and complexity of the work performed and should adjust for the quality level of the output. For acquisition tasks, this might include timely award, timely delivery, fair and reasonable prices, or customer satisfaction (Black, 1995; Sorber and Straight, 1995).

The second step is to project workload into the future. Bulmash, Chhinzer, and Speers (2010) identify several workload factors, also known as demand drivers, that influence future workload:

- general business environment—macroeconomic, legislative, and competitive pressures
- an organization's strategic goals and plans
- projected demand for products or services—at both the organization and the business unit level
- budget projections and financial resource availability
- new potential business opportunities.

Projections of future workload may rely on quantitative methods (for example, time-series analysis of sales data) or qualitative managerial judgment. In the case of DoD, such projections may also be informed by the planning process. Techniques vary in the number of demand drivers used to identify future workload.

The third step is to project worker productivity (estimated in Step 1) into the future and apply it to the future workload (from Step 2) in order to ultimately project required future workforce size. Most projec-

---

[1]   Various contracting organizations within DoD have workload models that use key performance indexes (i.e., characteristics of the workload) to relate workload to workforce size. For example, four primary performance indexes used in the Army Material Systems Analysis Agency (AMSAA) are contract actions, solicitations, ratio of competitive to noncompetitive actions, and the number of acquisition systems managed. The Air Force Manpower Standard uses dollars obligated and total actions completed as measures but also recognizes that large dollar actions are more complex than small dollar actions (Reed, 2011).

tion approaches involve some sort of assumption (implicit or explicit) about the correct level of productivity to be applied into the future and do so with varying degrees of sophistication and access to historical data. Options include assuming that current productivity levels continue, extrapolating historical trends in productivity, developing an "idealized" benchmark for productivity, and using qualitative judgment. Qualitative judgment is able to pick up changes in productivity caused by anticipated organizational/job design and administrative changes. For the rest of this chapter, we briefly discuss specific techniques and differences in the assumptions made by each method in translating workload and productivity projections into the number of required workers.

Projecting Future Workforce Demand: Quantitative Techniques

Ratio Analysis

Both the most simplistic and the most accessible technique, ratio analysis estimates future demand based on ratios between assumed demand drivers (number of items manufactured, number of clients served) and the total number of workers required. These ratios are based on current data and do not require significant historical data collection (Bulmash, Chhinzer, and Speers, 2010). This technique applies the *current* productivity ratio to future projections of the workload. For example, a private company may use the ratio of revenue to number of workers as a guide to predicting demand. Suppose that in 2012, a company generated $100,000 of revenue with 100 workers, which translates to a ratio of 1,000:1. If revenues are expected to increase to $200,000 in the following year, then ratio analysis would estimate a requirement of 200 workers. This technique can also inform the composition of workers, whether this is the mix of supervisor/laborer or military/civilian. For example, if 30 percent of 100 workers are currently supervisors, then with 200 workers, the company would require 60 supervisors. The key assumption of ratio analysis is that the current ratio remains fixed in the future. However, in reality, ratios may change over time because of changes in the composition of the workforce, company reorganization, and economies of scale. In such cases, ratio analysis may not be the best option.

Time-Series Analysis

Time-series analysis builds upon the reasoning of ratio analysis by tracking a ratio over a number of time periods in order to incorporate historical trends and changes in productivity. This technique assumes that *historical* workload and *historical* productivity are indicative of future workload and future productivity. In an example of a hotel chain, the demand drivers might be the number of hotel rooms and the percentage occupancy. Using historical data on the number of rooms occupied and the size of the housekeeping workforce, a hotel manager can calculate a historical ratio or performance index, which would be the number of rooms a housekeeper can clean in a day. Suppose that the hotel manager determines that each housekeeper can clean 20 rooms in a day, and historical tracking projects 100 percent occupancy in the summer and 60 percent occupancy in the winter. In a hotel with 100 rooms, the hotel manager would then forecast a demand for five housekeepers in the summer and three in the winter (Bulmash, Chhinzer, and Speers, 2010).

The primary strength of time-series analysis is its easy accessibility and implementation using spreadsheets. Using a time series to project the productivity ratio and workload is useful in identifying long-term trends, seasonal effects, business cycle effects, turning points, and random movement resulting from natural events and human actions (Meehan and Ahmed, 1990).[2] However, time-series analysis is limited to tracking only one ratio or performance index over time.

---

[2] Three common ways to smooth out short-run fluctuations and make forecasts are to apply moving averages, exponential smoothing, or Box-Jenkins estimation to time-series data (Bechet and Maki, 1987). While a moving average only takes into account a limited set of past data points, exponential smoothing takes into account all past data, and Box-Jenkins models a time series where past values explicitly affect current values.

Regression Analysis

Regression analysis is based on the statistical relationship between *multiple* productivity ratios and demand drivers tracked over time (independent variables) and the number of workers demanded (dependent variable). Independent variables may be relevant to the specific organization, to the industry to which the organization belongs (technology utilization, outsourcing), and to broad macroeconomic factors (interest rates, federal government budget). Like ratio analysis, regression analysis assumes that the relationship between demand drivers, productivity ratios, and the workforce will remain stable over time.

For example, Meehan and Ahmed (1990) use multiple regression demand models to forecast total staffing requirements, as well as requirements for certain categories of employees, in an electrical utility company—the dependent variables. Independent variables unique to the organization are selected to capture production volume (kilowatt hours of electricity generated, amount of assets in the net electrical plant) and revenue (sales revenue, net operating revenue). Certain budgeted expenses for office space rental, equipment, and travel are not appropriate as independent variables because they are the direct result of the total number of employees. However, the budget for outside services (consultants) is included as an independent variable because it is useful in forecasting future workload, and the model finds a significant decrease in total staffing requirements as the expenses for contracted services and consultants increase.

Once developed, regression models are straightforward to update and can handle large fluctuations well as long as the independent variables adequately reflect changes in organizational direction (Meehan and Ahmed, 1990). In general, regression models are particularly well-suited for mature organizations with relatively stable workforces and external environments. Regression models may also be able to inform the appropriate composition of workers by estimating the required number of one type of worker based on the required number of another type of worker. However, such models do require detailed historical data on multiple variables, and if the focus of the model needs to be changed for a particular subpopulation, a new model would have to be developed.

Regression models are also able to distinguish between different groups within an organization and to make specific demand forecasts based on mission and support functions unique to each group. Hinrichs and Morrison (1980) used a stepwise regression approach to forecast staffing demand for three functions in Navy research and development laboratories. The model assumes that the amount of workers demanded depends on the type of work performed. In the finance function, workload drivers used as independent variables include the total budget for the division, the number of travel requests processed, and the number of projects being accounted for. In the personnel function, workload drivers are the number of new hires in a given period, the number of promotions, the number of wage and salary classifications, and a summary count of the number of personnel actions in a set time period. For the purchase and supply function, independent variables are the number of items maintained and stored in the warehouse, the number of requisition stubs processed, and the number of contracts written. Their stepwise regression analysis uses a forward selection approach, where they start with no variables in the model, and each additional independent variable is tested using a model comparison criterion to ensure that adding the variable improves the model. Variables are added until no further improvements are generated.

Another example is the Health Resources and Services Administration's physician demand model, which estimates the number of doctors that society will likely employ given current utilization patterns and changing demographics. The main independent variables are detailed physician-to-population ratios; population projections by age, sex, and metropolitan or nonmetropolitan location; and projected insurance distributions by insurance type, age, sex, and metropolitan or nonmetropolitan location. A criticism of regression analysis in this context is that because it extrapolates current health care utilization and service delivery patterns, inequalities in the present system are perpetuated into future requirements (U.S. Department of Health and Human Services, 2008). In fact, the main point of caution for regression analysis is understanding that current workforce requirements should not always be assumed to be optimal, especially in situations when organizations undergo rapid change.

Benchmarking Analysis

Benchmarking analysis is an approach in which a certain gold standard or optimal numbers of workers are identified and then extrapolated to a new population. This is a different way of identifying a productivity ratio; whereas the other examples are based on current or historical patterns, this is based on *exemplars*. For example, Pinfield and McShane (1987) derive future demand for teachers by applying a "target" student-teacher ratio. Benchmarking analysis is often conducted in conjunction with reengineering activities within an organization that seek to achieve process improvements and productivity gains (Ward, 1996). In this case, an organization may attempt to detail components of work activities and arrive at a hypothetical "optimal" standard. For example, the Committee on the Costs of Medical Care determined a requirement of 140.5 physicians per 100,000 population (U.S. Department of Health and Human Services, 2008). It reached this ratio by estimating the incidence of disease, the expected number of patient-doctor encounters per disease incidence, the average amount of physician time per encounter, and the average total patient time per physician each year. Other examples of benchmarks include physician staffing ratios in health maintenance organizations and in other countries (Weiner, 2004).

This approach assumes that the benchmark standard identified represents an optimal requirement for the population or organizational segment to which it is being applied. In a large organization in which there are a number of similar subunits, such as a school district with many schools or a retail corporation with a number of similar local outlets, benchmarking may be straightforward to apply. In other situations, challenges in applying this method may arise. In the case of health care, for instance, the delivery system may be fundamentally different in the benchmarking entity than in the population of interest. Primary care physicians often play very different roles in the United States than they do in other countries (U.S. Department of Health and Human Services, 2008).

Input-Output Modeling

Input-output models translate activities of an organization into workforce demand requirements. The first step is to split the total amount of value that an organization produces into values from various categories of activities, such as recruiting, training, medical, procurement, logistics, transportation, facilities management, etc. Simple rules are used to characterize relationships between these categories; generally, these relationships are assumed to be linear, which means perfect substitutability of inputs. The value of each activity category is used as a proxy for the cost of labor in producing that activity. These rules are then applied together to determine how external demands on an organization's activities affect the number of workers required to perform these activities.

This technique has been used by the Total Army Analysis (TAA) and the Generating Force-to-Operator (GTO) models. TAA derives demand requirements for combat units from activities within major combat operations plans. In an analogous way, GTO translates activities supporting the Army operating force into requirements for the Army generating force.

Box 4.1: Generating Force-to-Operator Tool

The GTO tool is an input-output model developed by RAND to forecast manpower size requirements (the inputs) within the Army generating force (Camm et al., 2011). The Army generating force delivers outputs of personnel, material, and information assets, as well as direct support goods and services, to the deployable forces within the operational Army. The model tracks activities in the generating force and associates them with value to users in the operational Army and to other users within the generating force. GTO assumes that the user value of each activity's output is a proxy for the cost of producing that activity, which in turn is a proxy for the cost of labor. Because many activities within the generating force are interrelated, a matrix is used to represent the value added from one activity to another. The end result of the model is an estimation of how a change in external demand from the operational Army would affect the level of demand for each

Box 4.1—continued

activity within the generating force, which would affect the total workforce size requirement of the generating force.

The inherent structure of the input-output model affords certain advantages and disadvantages. It is important to recognize that a standard input-output model does not allow any surplus (i.e., the user value of production must equal the cost of production in any activity). Thus, the standard model does not capture situations where efforts to reduce the cost of an activity might yield net benefits. However, an advantage is that it allows the cost of producing any activity to be used as a measure of the user value of its output. This is particularly beneficial in a setting where there are no markets to inform the value of outputs. Another feature of the GTO model that can be considered both an advantage and a disadvantage is its assumption of steady-state conditions. In a steady state, costs and values are equal, so the model does not require empirical measures of values of key outputs of the generating force, as long as the costs of production are known. A disadvantage of this feature is that it makes GTO more useful when applied to longer time horizons (on the order of five years or more), where investment flows are closely aligned with benefits, but not appropriate for year-to-year application.

At least two potential applications for the GTO model are possible. The simplest application is providing senior Army leadership with better visibility of the reason each component of the generating force exists and the costs of serving operational users inside the Army. In addition, the GTO model has the ability to support activity-based budgeting—i.e., budgeting based on the expected level of activity output, in order to address uncertainties about the future environment of the Army.

Projecting Future Workforce Demand: Qualitative Techniques

An alternative approach to quantitative techniques involves gathering and synthesizing individual judgments—typically from managers, planners, or experts—about future demand. In such cases, it is difficult to distinguish the process of gathering data from the analysis of such data. For example, if an organization surveys its managers to ask how many employees each manager will need next year, then one might argue that each manager analyzes his or her workforce demand individually, and the survey is simply a tool for gathering data on demand. However, there is typically some coordination or other qualitative analysis involved in aggregating individuals' estimates or in reconciling various expert or manager opinions. Therefore, we discuss qualitative techniques for gathering judgments about demand here, rather than in the following chapters on data collection.

Direct Managerial Survey

Within workforce planning, one of the most commonly practiced approaches is to project workforce demand using direct managerial judgment (Ward, 1996). In this approach, each manager will prepare a forecast of the demand for employees in the skill groups or job families in his or her area. These forecasts include not only current head count requirements but also a best-guess estimate of how these head counts may change due to anticipated productivity changes in

1. technology and systems
2. development, acquisition, or logistic processes
3. the organization itself
4. personnel policies.

The total future estimate comes from aggregating each separate forecast. An important feature of using manager judgment directly is that each manager has maximum flexibility in determining what staffing level is necessary in meeting workplace objectives and in distinguishing between critical and noncritical skills. Unfortunately, there will be inconsistencies across managers in effort spent providing input and ability to intuitively forecast workforce requirements. Because interviews and surveys depend on self-reported data rather than objectively measured data, they may be biased, especially toward recent work.

Delphi Method/ExpertLens

The best known qualitative technique for projecting future demand is the Delphi method, which was developed by RAND as a more formalized approach to eliciting and integrating expert opinion (Dalkey and Helmer-Hirschberg, 1962). It follows an iterative process in which experts provide feedback on each other's views with the goal of eventually leading to a dependable consensus of opinion. By design, experts are restricted from engaging in direct face-to-face communication in order to minimize possibly detrimental group interaction aspects, such as the bandwagon effect of majority opinion, unwillingness to abandon publicly stated positions, and social persuasion (Gatewood and Gatewood, 1983).

Application of the Delphi method follows a routine set of steps:

1. A panel of experts is identified from a pool of unit heads and human resource managers.
2. Each expert submits a demand forecast, which details information sources and assumptions used. In addition to sales, production, experience, education, and turnover levels of the workforce within the organization, experts also rely on economic, social, legal, demographic, and technological conditions outside the organization (Bulmash, Chhinzer, and Speers, 2010).
3. The forecasts are gathered and summarized by the human resources planning group, which sends the aggregated results back to the panel of experts.
4. Experts individually reevaluate their forecasts in light of the information provided in the summaries.

Steps 2 through 4 are repeated until the expert forecasts converge. Each iteration gives the experts an opportunity to understand their relative positions and gain valuable feedback from other experts in a controlled, standardized, non-interactive manner. The narrowing of differences generally takes three to five rounds (Bulmash, Chhinzer, and Speers, 2010).

The main criticisms of the Delphi method can be generalized to almost any qualitative expert elicitation method. First, there is a dependency on the subjective forecasts of the particular judges selected, and there is difficulty in assessing the degree of expertise incorporated in the forecast (Gatewood and Gatewood, 1983). Second, results may be sensitive to ambiguity in phrasing of the data collection questionnaire (Makridakis and Wheelwright, 1978).

Despite these criticisms, because of the direct involvement of organization members in the forecasting process, forecasts arising from the Delphi method are often well-received within the organization under study. In fact, they have the potential to outperform quantitative techniques. In a study by Milkovich, Annoni, and Mahoney (1972), a demand forecast from the Delphi method was compared against a forecast from a simple regression model and validated using the actual number of workers hired in the following year. In their application of the Delphi method, seven company managers were asked to estimate the number of buyers the firm would need one year into the future, and after five rounds, the median estimate and interquartile range were determined. The study results indicated closer agreement between the Delphi estimate and the actual number of buyers hired than between the regression forecast and the actual number of buyers hired. Similarly, Basu and Schroeder (1977) compared a five-year Delphi forecast using 23 key organization managers against both unstructured, directed managerial surveys and quantitative forecasts using regression analysis and exponential smoothing. After being validated against actual sales results, errors of 0.3 to 4 percent were reported for Delphi, while errors of about 20 percent were reported for unstructured managerial surveys, and errors of 10 to 15 percent were reported for the quantitative techniques.

The Delphi method is particularly useful for situations with limited or uncertain historical data, changing government policy, specific educational patterns, new technology leading to evolving skill levels, and dynamic changes in work processes, which would affect worker productivity (Gatewood and Gatewood, 1983). It is adept at answering a specific, one-dimensional question. For more complex forecasts involving multiple jobs or personnel classes, the Delphi method can serve as a source of inputs for a quantitative model—this will be discussed further in this chapter's section on combined qualitative and quantitative techniques.

In addition, another possible Delphi-type implementation is the ExpertLens system, also developed by RAND (Dalal et al., 2011). ExpertLens is an online platform that allows the Delphi method to be used by experts in different locations who participate at a time that is convenient for them. Rather than require these experts to reach consensus, ExpertLens statistically analyzes these expert opinions to understand the overall group opinion.

Nominal Group Technique

In contrast to the arm's-length nature of the Delphi method, the NGT process allows for face-to-face interaction among a panel of experts (generally managers) to discuss an organizational issue. These issues are not limited to future workforce demand and can also include decisions about launching new products or processes, establishing sales targets, and managing change (Bulmash, Chhinzer, and Speers, 2010).

NGT was developed by Delbecq and Van de Ven (1971) in order to enhance group brainstorming of ideas, and it follows five steps:

1. A facilitator solicits experts and explains the purpose and procedure of the meeting. Each expert is asked the same specific question. (For example, "what is your forecast of future workforce demand, and what are the causes of expected changes in demand?")

2. Independently, each expert generates ideas and writes down his or her answer to the question.

3. Experts meet face to face to individually present their answers, which are recorded to allow for later comparison. Interruption or discussion is discouraged during this step, but experts are encouraged to write down any new ideas that arise from what others have shared.

4. After all experts have presented, the facilitator encourages group discussion and clarifying questions. During this time, the group may suggest new answers or combine existing answers.

5. Each expert will anonymously vote on rankings of the answers. The facilitator then uses the highest-ranked answer as the demand estimate.

NGT can be iterative if the rankings are too close for distinguishing a best estimate. In that case, Steps 4 and 5 would be repeated. The rationale for this procedure is that the number of ideas generated by "nominal groups" (i.e., experts generating answers silently and independently, prior to group discussion) is greater than the number of ideas generated by fully interacting groups (Delbecq and Van de Ven, 1971). Studies on group brainstorming have shown that an increased number of heterogeneous ideas leads to higher-quality decisions and greater originality (Taylor, Berry, and Block, 1958).

Just like the Delphi method, NGT avoids certain negative aspects of group interaction by ensuring equal participation and providing built-in mechanisms to protect against criticism. It is useful when certain group members are particularly vocal and others may be reluctant to create conflict. In fact, because of the inflexible nature of NGT, it requires a degree of conformity on the part of the experts and only allows for dealing with one specific question at a time. The very mechanical structure of NGT may also limit the spontaneity of idea generation and constrain the cross-fertilization of ideas, which are benefits of a normal (not nominal) group interaction. Another disadvantage is the amount of time required in arranging and performing the procedure of an in-person expert panel (Centers for Disease Control and Prevention, 2006).

Scenario Analysis
Unlike all previously discussed qualitative techniques, where the ultimate product is a single demand scenario, scenario analysis produces multiple estimates of demand. Each estimate is contingent on a different set of assumptions about the organization's economic outlook. For example, forecasts may be contingent upon three different levels of growth: a status quo scenario with 0-percent firm output growth, an optimistic scenario with 5-percent output growth, and a pessimistic scenario with a 5-percent output decline (Bulmash, Chhinzer, and

Speers, 2010). A range of these scenarios is generated through face-to-face expert brainstorming sessions, and the interactive nature of expert discussion encourages innovative thinking and consideration of the future that might be missed in other approaches.

Peter Schwartz's *The Art of the Long View* (1960) describes tools to create scenario building blocks and provides examples of scenario planning conducted at companies and institutions, including Royal Dutch/Shell, BellSouth, Pacific Gas & Electric, the Environmental Protection Agency, and the International Stock Exchange. This technique recognizes the high level of uncertainty about the future and the high number of factors that can affect demand. These factors may be internal changes (for instance, productivity or technological changes) or external changes (for instance, changes in the economic, legislative, or competitive environment), and the combination of factors produces a wide range of plausible futures. For example, RAND's Robust Decision Making approach works toward exploring the entire range of possibilities and identifying the most influential underlying drivers (Lempert, Popper, and Bankes, 2003). Thus, scenario analysis is particularly good for dynamic organizations experiencing large changes, where the past is not the best predictor of the future. However, there is no consideration of any parameters of measurement accuracy, such as confidence intervals, standard errors, nonresponse rates, reporting errors, and sample size. While scenario analysis is able to explore the entire range of possible scenarios, it is not meant to assign probabilities to each scenario, and therefore it is less effective at providing a single expected value for workforce demand.

Projecting Future Demand: Combining Qualitative and Quantitative Techniques

In real-world application, organizations are not constrained to using only quantitative or qualitative techniques, and, in fact, they often use approaches that combine both. Quantitative techniques are often hampered by a lack of systematic data collection, which we discuss in more detail in the following chapter. Qualitative methods do not require historical data, but they do require input from managers, planners, or experts, which may be difficult or costly to acquire. Such methods may also suffer from validity issues because of their subjective nature. In response to the dual challenges posed by both quantitative and qualitative demand projection techniques, a trend in the evolution of demand forecasting is applying a combination of such techniques. In this section, we describe broadly two main types of approaches that are often seen in practice: top-down and bottom-up. We also briefly discuss a specific technique that has never been applied but could potentially be useful.

Top-Down

A top-down approach begins with historical data of total staffing levels and uses regression analysis to derive a relationship between the number of workers required and measures of workload (Chan, Moore, and Chenoweth, 2012). Just as with previously discussed regression models, workload is projected into the future using historical data on demand drivers, assuming that job processes do not change appreciably. A traditional regression analysis would describe the workload in quantitative terms (for instance, number of contract actions, number of engineering changes, procurement dollars). However, quantitative demand drivers may be insufficient in accurately describing workload. A demand driver such as the number of contracts awarded would not account for fundamental differences in effort required to develop and award various contracts. For example, an office writing a fixed-price, sole-source contract would have a different workload than an office writing an incentive-based, competitive contract. An alternative is to take a more qualitative approach to describing workload.

Consisting of both quantitative and qualitative elements, the Sustainment and Acquisition Composite Model (SACOM) is a commonly cited top-down approach to estimating the workforce size requirements for weapon system acquisition program offices. The model is proprietary to a private company, Dayton Aerospace Inc. The company accounts for fundamental differences in workload by identifying 25 program characteristics in five general categories: the quantity and level of required reporting, the volatility of user requirements, the magnitude of contracting activity, the amount of interaction with other government agencies, and the amount of management and technical oversight required (Vernez et al., 2007). For every program office, each characteristic is scored on a 1 to 5 scale through structured interviews with managers, and these characteristics serve as workload factors. The tool was created in 2001 and has been validated on various subpopulations in the Air Force, such as Aircraft, Electronics, Munitions, and Hardware. It has been supplanted by the Acquisition/Sustainment Unit (ASU) model.

In general, top-down models require less data than bottom-up models and are easier to construct. Historical staffing data, including measures of skill level and experience, are readily available. However, just as with traditional regression analysis, this approach assumes that historical staffing-to-workload ratios are appropriate and will hold in the future. When organizational processes change, new historical staffing data must be compiled in order to update the model. In addition, there is no visibility into reasons for a given staffing level. A final weakness is that this approach may also inadvertently capture staffing associated with overhead functions.

Box 4.2: Acquisition/Sustainment Unit Model

The Air Force Manpower Agency developed the ASU model in 2008 in response to concerns over the subjectivity of scoring involved with the proprietary Dayton Aerospace SACOM model. The ASU model takes a top-down approach to modeling demand requirements for acquisition program offices, using linear regressions based on historical totals. ASU is used to project total staffing levels required for Air Force acquisition program offices, with the allocation of specialties and grades of personnel based on historical average percentages.

The most prominent feature of ASU is that it makes distinctions between the types of goods or services being acquired. ASU includes six different types of procurement programs, and each is treated separately within ASU with a different set of demand drivers. Table 4.1 lists the six programs and summarizes the demand drivers for each type of program. ASU was first built by qualitatively identifying possible demand drivers for each type of program. At one point, more than 70 possible demand drivers were considered, and eventually statistical tests were conducted on various combinations of drivers to narrow them down to two or three per program.

Box 4.2—continued

    While ASU has the advantage of being simple to run with readily available data, a possible disadvantage is that the model is driven by historical data based on manpower requirements of older systems. As new technology will replace old systems in the future, it is questionable how well the model will perform going forward. In addition, the model was originally intended to model 14 procurement programs. FY 2006 data were used to calibrate the model, and it was then compared to actual FY 2007 staffing levels for validation. Unfortunately, out of the 14 programs, only the six programs currently included in ASU "passed" (they had a discrepancy of less than 20 percent between predicted and actual staffing levels). The remaining eight procurement programs (Acquisition of Communications and Radar, Software, Space, Technology and Accessories, Sustainment of Munitions, Radar, Support, and Targets) are currently the subjects of ongoing study.

Table 4.1
Procurement Program Demand Drivers in the ASU Model

Type of Procurement Program	Demand Drivers
Acquisition Aircraft	• Budgeted dollars • Contract awards • Modifications
Acquisition Munitions	• Budgeted dollars • Certification actions • Technical order pages
Sustainment Aircraft	• Budgeted dollars • Engineering assessments
Sustainment Aircraft Components	• Engineering actions • Contract modifications
Sustainment Communications	• Budgeted dollars • Engineering actions
Sustainment Accessories	• Budgeted dollars • Engineering actions

Bottom-Up

A bottom-up approach begins with detailed estimates of the labor required for each piece of work and then aggregates the estimates to calculate the total staffing level required. Examples of this approach include the AMSAA Acquisition Center Standard, the Air Force Workload Assessment Model (WAM), the Navy's Time to Produce (TTP) model, and the Censeo Procurement Workload Analysis Model (PWAM) (Chan, Moore, and Chenoweth, 2012). In a contracting setting, this would entail estimating the labor hours to perform various tasks in issuing and managing contracts. Collecting data on the time required for each task usually relies on a combination of quantitative and qualitative methods. When possible, time studies are conducted, in which evaluators observe tasks performed and directly measure the amount of labor required. However, this often makes data collection itself overly burdensome, and an alternative method is to qualitatively ask managers to estimate labor times, using interviews, panels, and surveys.

The bottom-up approach is less dependent than the top-down approach on historical staffing to guide future forecasts of the "right" level of staffing, although it is still dependent on historical processes. By providing a task-by-task accounting of the work, it is more transparent as to how workforce size requirements are estimated. This also allows for easier updating when processes change and productivity increases, by directly updating the individual task times.

Unlike the top-down approach, in which data on aggregate workload and workforce size are likely available, a disadvantage of the bottom-up approach is that special data collection is often required. As an example, WAM is particularly labor-intensive, with a manual data call each year with periodic validation of the hours attributed to workload types. In addition, deciding the appropriate level of detail in modeling individual tasks is critical. In order to accurately forecast demand, an attempt must be made to capture all of the tasks performed and to account for all the time of each worker.

Box 4.3: Censeo Procurement Workload Analysis Model

The Censeo Consulting Group built the Procurement Workload Analysis Model (PWAM) for the U.S. Army in 2010 (Chan, Moore, and Chenoweth, 2012). The model's purpose is to estimate the contracting officer personnel required to execute changes in workload and to predict the administrative lead time needed to award a contract. More specifically, the model estimates the *incremental* staffing requirements associated with additional contracts, rather than *total* staffing requirements. It takes a bottom-up approach, starting with labor requirements for a single contract. The model consists of two spreadsheets: a micro model, which estimates staffing and lead time for each contract, and a macro model, which aggregates all contracts to estimate total staffing requirements. For each contract within the micro model, data were generated through surveys asking contracting offices to pick any three recent contracts that they had worked on and recall the amount of time necessary to complete tasks associated with each contract. For each task, both the "actual" time and the "ideal" time were elicited. The survey also asked for contract characteristics to distinguish between different types of contracts and different types of items being purchased. The characteristics are mission objective, contract type, commercial type, procurement method, dollar value, pricing structure, incentive fees, and requirements complexity. The micro model uses a regression model to estimate the relationship between the number of hours of labor required (dependent variable) and contract characteristics (independent variables). Then the macro model takes the amount of time required for each contract and the number of types of contracts the organization expects to handle in a year to provide an aggregate estimate for the number of contracting officers required.

The main criticism of the PWAM model is that it is dependent on self-reported survey data due to the lack of actual historical data on time spent per contract. In addition, because the survey respondents were able to select any three contracts to report on, the model may suffer from selection bias. Without a second source of data for comparison, it is difficult to validate the reliability of the survey data.

Causal Cross-Impact Analysis

Cross-impact analysis was developed by RAND to use expert judgment as an input for a quantitative simulation model (Helmer, 1977). Forecasting is based on perceptions about how future events may interact. Utilizing this technique requires populating two sets of data. The first set, common to other techniques, describes how individual events in isolation affect the estimated variable. The second set, unique to this technique, consists of a cross-impact matrix, which describes how each event affects other events. Each element in the matrix is a conditional probability, and the matrix encompasses every possible interaction between events. The information for these two sets of data is generally obtained from qualitative expert elicitation, such as by the Delphi method, and then fed as inputs into a quantitative computer simulation model. Final output consists of a variety of scenarios, each estimating a particular set of events and associated estimates, as well as a sensitivity analysis, which determines the extent to which estimates are affected by changes in inputs.

Because cross-impact analysis is more costly and complex than direct estimation using the Delphi method, no actual application of this technique to workforce demand forecasting has been identified in the literature. However, Gatewood and Gatewood (1983) cite this method as a potential future technique for demand forecasting. In this case, the variable estimated would be the number of workers required for a certain job class, and model events could include work process changes, technological changes, organizational plans and policies, or company strategic decisions.

A strength of cross-impact analysis is the application of statistical analysis to otherwise purely qualitative analysis. Mathematical formulae are used to define probability distributions of the variable being forecast, calculate upper and lower bounds for events and trends, and adjust for cross-impacts. The use of simulations allows for easy validation in broad settings. A weakness of this technique comes from the inflexibility when dealing with a variety of events. Because interaction effects are manifested in terms of a single entry in a matrix, complex interactions are boiled down to a simple number. Impacts can only be applied to the next time period, not across multiple periods, and there is only a binary consideration of whether or not an event occurs, without taking into account the magnitude of the event.

CHAPTER FIVE

Availability of Data for Workforce Analysis in DoD

Data are a critical input into the supply and demand models described in Chapters Three and Four. In this chapter, we briefly discuss some variables that are commonly used in supply and demand analysis, and we provide an overview of the main types of data sources used in supply and demand analysis. We then turn to a detailed analysis of the availability of data sources within DoD.

Variables Commonly Used in Workforce Analysis

For projecting internal or external supply, a key consideration involves identifying the variables on which to base projections. A very basic model might project one separation rate and apply it to all employees in the organization. More sophisticated models may recognize that separation rates often vary by gender, years of service, or other worker characteristics and thus apply different rates to different groups. For example, the RAND Inventory Model calculates separation and new-hire rates by YORE and by retirement plan. Similarly, a regression model could project different separation rates for different groups of workers by including worker characteristics as explanatory variables in the estimation.

Previous work indicates that employee age, gender, length of service, skills, and responsibilities are important factors in predicting separation rates (Edwards, 1983). For U.S. government employees, total years of service as a federal employee is also an important factor, as many employees choose to leave immediately after becoming retirement-eligible (Gates et al., 2008).

Many supply models rely on a common set of employee characteristics, such as age, education, and occupation. These variables are often collected as part of the human resources process and are thus already available for supply analyses.

External variables may also affect new-hire and separation rates. A lower unemployment rate may increase separation rates, as employees are more likely to have outside opportunities, and may decrease new-hire rates, as fewer potential employees accept offers. Other factors that could affect external supply or separations (adapted from Australian Public Service Commission, 2011) include

- general economic conditions, including unemployment rates
- demographic trends (of the internal and the external workforce)
- workforce participation rates
- competitor demand and job vacancy rates in the external labor market
- social trends (for example, increased worker mobility)
- education, skill, and training patterns of the local workforce
- government policies that affect the ability to hire or retain workers.

Data on general economic conditions, demographic trends, workforce participation rates, job vacancies in the external labor market, and education can typically be obtained from sources such as the U.S. Census, the Bureau of Labor Statistics, and the Department of Education (or similar state or local agencies). These data may be at a relatively aggregate level; the Bureau of Labor Statistics provides the number of job openings by region and by broad industry (for example, durable goods manufacturing). More disaggregated data, or data on other factors, may be available through industry reports, expert opinion solicitation, or other sources.

In contrast to supply projections, which rely on readily available data, quantitative demand projections are often hampered by a lack of systematic data collection. Basic demand models, such as ratio models, might rely only on data about an organization's sales and its employee head count, which might already be available. However, if managers want to conduct more sophisticated analyses, such as regression-based models linking workload drivers and workforce size for a particular function or division, then it is critical to identify the correct demand drivers and measures of productivity. Such drivers are likely to be organization-specific, and it is important to consider workload factors that might become more important in the future. Identifying appropriate drivers, and measures of those drivers, requires careful forethought and organization. The process may be particularly challenging within complex organizations or for groups of employees who produce outputs that are difficult to measure. Once such drivers have been identified, collecting a sufficient amount of historical data takes time, and a small sample size will affect model accuracy.

One option for avoiding the need to identify and collect data on workload drivers would be to use qualitative demand projection methods. Strictly speaking, in this case the respondent performs the necessary analysis, so the only variable to be collected is the projected number of employees. However, it may be useful to elicit other information from managers or experts about projected workload factors or overall business conditions. Such information can serve to reconcile differing estimates, and to ensure that projections are consistent across business units.

Potential Data Sources for Workforce Analysis

There are a variety of potential data sources that can be used in creating supply and demand projections. Existing data sources can typically be grouped into three categories:

1. data generated and maintained by organizations on organizational or business unit outcomes (for example, sales), inputs, or workforce characteristics (for example, new hires or retirement)

2. member organization data (for example, information about the number of doctors registered with the American Medical Association)
3. broader data or information (for example, data about the economy or the labor force from the Bureau of Labor Statistics).

Many organizations retain rich data on employee hiring, promotion, retention, and retirement. Such employee datasets are frequently used to characterize employee flows into, within, and out of organizations, and to populate supply projection models (Bechet, 1994). As we discuss in more detail below, many components within DoD maintain personnel data systems that track historical employee information. Organizations often maintain information on such historical workload factors as sales, production, or number of contracts, which may be linked with personnel data to analyze employee demand.

Workforce planning models often draw on member organization data, particularly for the health care workforce. For example, many physician workforce models use data from the American Medical Association regarding the numbers, specialties, and characteristics of physicians, as well as retirement rates, and create estimates of future physician supply from enrollment data provided by the American Association of Medical Colleges (see, for example, U.S. Department of Health and Human Services, 2008).

Broader population and economic data can be gathered from a variety of sources, including the U.S. Census Bureau, the Bureau of Labor Statistics, and the Bureau of Economic Analysis. For example, the physician workforce can be modeled as a function of population size, demographic characteristics, or economic characteristics, which can be gathered from the U.S. Census Bureau or other sources (Cooper et al., 2002; U.S. Department of Health and Human Services, 2008). Epidemiological data on incidence rates of certain diseases may also be used in projecting physician workforce demand (Lee, Jackson, and Relles, 1995).

Some workforce planning exercises, particularly demand projections, require supplementing existing data with newly collected data.

Such data are typically specific to the organization in question or to the industry in which it operates. Surveys and interviews are often used in collecting such data. For example, Vernez et al. (2007) use Air Force Manpower data to identify the composition of the acquisition workforce but suggest using surveys of line managers to gather information on future workforce requirements under various scenarios. Masi et al. (2009) combine administrative data from HRC with survey data regarding worker requirements, interviews with subject matter experts, and publicly available data on the local workforce in studying gaps between HRC workforce requirements and labor supply in Fort Knox. The physician supply model discussed above combines professional member organization data on the number of physicians with existing surveys on hours worked and productivity (U.S. Department of Health and Human Services, 2008). Industry-level growth estimates might also be used to project potential sales for an organization, and thus worker demand.

Overview of Existing Data Availability in DoD

In this section, we summarize our findings from a review of major data systems used within DoD. Our review revealed many data systems, including systems that have been in place for a number of years (often referred to as "legacy" systems), as well as those that have recently been rolled out or are under development. Our goal is not to provide an exhaustive list of these data systems in DoD, but rather to focus on relatively high-level data sources. While we recognize that richer data may be collected within parts of DoD, the goal of our analysis is to identify data sources that can be helpful in DoD-wide efforts. We view data systems that are already used by large groups within DoD as more likely to meet this goal.

Workforce data systems in DoD typically fall within one of two broad areas. Personnel systems contain information about the current workforce ("faces") and can be viewed as representing current supply. Manpower systems contain information about requirements or authorizations ("spaces") and can be viewed as representing current (or future) demand.

To view the workforce using a Total Force concept, DoD managers will need information on the military, civilian, and contractor workforces. Below, we consider the availability of data systems for each of these workforces, with an emphasis on the civilian and contractor workforces. For each of these workforces, we discuss the availability of personnel inventories, as well as manpower requirements or authorization counts. We then turn to the question of what data are collected on variables related to competencies, both in terms of competency levels of the current workforce and in terms of competency requirements for positions. Given that information about competencies remains limited to certain functions and occupations (including the Acquisition Workforce, as we discuss in more detail below), we cast a fairly wide net, including such information as education, languages, and performance ratings that appear in the data sources we reviewed. Finally, to illustrate the types of available data, we provide a closer look into the Air Force's manpower data system.

Civilian Data

There are many sources of civilian data counts on both the personnel and manpower sides. We begin by discussing the DoD-wide civilian personnel data system, as well as some of the personnel and manpower systems used by large services and agencies. We then consider data on competencies, which are far less easily found both at the DoD-wide and service- or agency-specific levels.

Personnel Inventory

The DCPDS was created in 1999 with the integration of ten separate sources of data into a single system. DCPDS collects a wide range of demographic and job-related information on all DoD civilian employees, including data on occupation, career history, wage grade, base location, and years of service.

A number of systems draw on DCPDS data. At the DoD-wide level, the Customer Support Units at each DoD Human Resources (HR) Regional Service Center draw on DCPDS data to process civilian HR actions. Similarly, the Corporate Management Information System (CMIS) contains a variety of tools to assist users in accessing DCPDS data (DoD, 2010). In addition, the Defense Manpower Data Center (DMDC) periodically extracts data from the DCPDS to create a range of files, including quarterly snapshots; such transactions as promotions, transfers, awards, and wage grade changes; and pay files (Gates, Eibner, and Keating, 2006).

Individual services and agencies also draw on DCPDS data to feed systems that are aimed at workforce management or analysis. For example, the Army Civilian Personnel System (HQ ACPERS) is used to support personnel reporting and management requirements. HQ ACPERS contains personnel records for appropriated fund and non-appropriated fund Army civilians and is populated using data from DCPDS and from non-Army systems that service Army employees. Similarly, forecasting models used by DLA (IWAPM) and the Army (CIVFORS) draw on quarterly updates of DCPDS data. Another workforce analysis tool, the AT&L Workforce Data Mart, accesses all acquisition workforce data collected from DCPDS, the Air Force's Military Personnel Data System (MilPDS), and other sources. DoD draws on Data Mart for a variety of statistics related to civilian and military acquisition personnel, ranging from simple counts to monitoring of certification rates (GAO, 2010).

A variety of more narrowly focused personnel systems also exist. For instance, MilPDS is an Oracle HR system that integrates a variety of subsystems and is used to manage personnel, adjust pay, and assign troops. MilPDS includes information about all active, retired, and reserve Air Force members. The Marine Corps maintains the Marine Corps Total Force System (MCTFS), which includes information about separations, pay, recruiting, and assignments. Both of these systems contain military personnel information, and MCTFS also includes civilian information.

Although an individual in a personnel inventory file may be explicitly linked with the position he or she occupies, that position information typically does not reflect manpower requirements or authorizations and hence workforce demand. The acquisition workforce person file contains a record for each individual (both military and civilian) who was included in the service or agency submissions made in accordance with DoD Instruction 5000.55. Each acquisition workforce (AW) person record includes an AW position code and can thus be linked to the position data. (Gates et al., 2013). Similarly, MilPDS also contains a position number that corresponds to a position identifier in the Air Force's requirements database (Manpower Programming and Execution System [MPES]). In most cases, however, manpower requirements and authorizations data are maintained separately from personnel and related position data. Below, we provide an overview of major manpower databases in DoD.

Manpower Requirements and Authorizations

Each of the major services has its own manpower database; these databases are typically updated as part of the force development process. For example, the Army uses its TAA process to determine a force structure that balances requirements against resource constraints (U.S. Department of the Army, 1995). During the TAA, the Army develops its Program Objective Memorandum force, which is subsequently submitted to OSD for approval (U.S. Army War College, 2011). The TAA process is supposed to identify not only military positions, but also civilian and contractor support (U.S. Department of the Army, 1995). Historically, the force structure has been documented in SAMAS, with each authorized unit recorded in The Army Authorization Document System (TAADS) document that specifies its mission, structure, personnel, and equipment authorizations. The Army is in the process of developing the Force Management System (FMS), which will replace SAMAS and TAADS and is slated to become the Army's only database for authorizations and requirements (U.S. Army War College, 2011). Similarly, the Air Force and Navy maintain their civilian and military requirements data in MPES and the Total Force Manpower Management System (TFMMS), respectively.

The manpower databases are used in a variety of applications and interfaces for facilitating analysis. For example, data from SAMAS feed into a number of applications and user interfaces, including the Civilian Manpower Integrated Costing System (a system for estimating civilian manpower costs) and FMSWeb (an online website facili-tating access to FMS data). FMSWeb has the capability to aggregate civilian manpower numbers by occupation, command, or UIC. In the Air Force, the Total Human Resource Managers' Information System (THRMIS) is web-based software that collects and aggregates data from multiple sources, including personnel and manpower databases. THRMIS aggregates the data into interactive statistical abstracts that are used by career field managers and Air Staff action officers to assess the state of functional communities (FCs) in the Air Force.[1]

Competencies

NDAA FY 2010 requires OUSD (P&R) to develop a strategic work-force plan that includes an assessment of the critical skills and com-petencies that will be required of the future civilian workforce and an inventory of critical skills and competencies in the existing work-force, thus allowing a gap analysis to be performed. DoDI 1400.25 Volume 250 indicates that the Deputy Assistant Secretary of Defense for Civilian Personnel Policy (DASD [CPP]) shall establish common taxonomies for competencies, as well as a five-point rating scale for competency proficiency levels.

DoD has made progress toward developing and assessing com-petencies for mission-critical occupations (MCOs) (GAO, 2014). For example, a DoD-wide team established a list of competencies for each of five occupational series pertaining to financial management: finan-cial management analyst, financial technician, financial manager, accountant, and auditor. The competencies are classified as technical, leadership, and business acumen competencies. Each of these com-petencies describes the requirements for three proficiency levels (U.S. Department of the Navy, 2009). Table 5.1 provides an example of com-petencies required for the 501 (Financial Management Analyst) occu-pational series.

---

[1] We also looked into the possibility that civilian requirements data might be available from the DoD Commercial Activities Management Information System (DCAMIS), a DoD-wide database that documents information associated with competitive sourcing studies. However, it appears that DCAMIS was taken offline in 2011 (GAO, 2011b).

Table 5.1
DoD Financial Management (501) Occupation Series and Competencies

Competency Category	Competency
Technical	• Accounting Concepts: Knowledge of general accounting procedures and processes, including budgetary and proprietary accounting
	• Budget Execution: Knowledge of funds' flow from higher headquarters to the executing activity level
	• Budget Formulation: Knowledge of the formulation of an activity budget and the relationship to the overall U.S. Department of the Navy budget
	• Financial Analysis: Knowledge of predictive and trend analysis, plan-to-actual comparisons, and other statistical methods
	• Financial Systems and Reporting: Knowledge of data derived from organizational financial management and reporting requirements
	• Financial Rules and Regulations: Knowledge of appropriations law and financial rules and regulations
Leadership	• Interpersonal skills
	• Integrity/honesty
	• Flexibility
	• Accountability
	• Develop others
	• Partnering
	• Strategic thinking
	• Political savvy
	• External awareness
	• Vision
Business Acumen	• Ability to communicate effectively, orally, and in writing
	• Ability to use computer software applications
	• Awareness of customer needs
	• Ability to solve problems
	• Ability to influence/negotiate

SOURCE: U.S. Department of the Navy, 2009.

Currently, information on competency requirements or competency levels among personnel is not systematically collected. DoD has developed a Defense Competency Assessment Tool to support competency gap analysis. DoD started using the tool in October 2013, and it was applied to the financial management community in April–May 2014 (GAO, 2014). The tool should allow each employee to be assigned certain competency requirements and to assess his or her proficiency with respect to that competency; supervisors will also be able to assess their employees' proficiency levels, and gaps between the two assessments will be highlighted (U.S. Department of the Navy, 2011).

Until the Competency Assessment Tool, or a similar tool, is widely used within DoD, some information about competencies, particularly on the personnel side, may be gleaned from existing data. The DCPDS data contain several variables that are related to competencies for current personnel. The variables available at a DoD-wide level cover basic information, such as education level and language proficiency. A performance rating (on a scale of 1 to 5) is also available, and some information about competency may be inferred from speed of promotion through pay grades, quality step increases, or cash awards, all of which are recorded in the DCPDS data.

However, Gates, Eibner, and Keating (2006) discuss three key limitations of the DCPDS dataset with respect to competency-related variables. First, while the system has the capacity to collect information on training and certification, there is no agency-wide requirement for recording such information and little incentive for local personnel offices to record or update it. In addition, the types of training recorded differ across components. Therefore, training data are variable and often missing. Second, DCPDS does not have data on the specific skills an individual possesses beyond language ability and what can be inferred from past and present occupation variables. Finally, the performance data in DCPDS are of some value, although the vast majority of individuals have the three highest rating scores. Steps were made in the last ten years to improve the performance rating system, but still less than 1 percent of personnel receive one of the two lowest scores.

Another potential source of competency data (albeit for a small fraction of civilian employees) is the Defense Talent Management

System for Senior Executive Service (SES) employees. DoD has defined core competencies for senior leaders, based on OPM guidance. Senior leaders and their supervisors then assess themselves with respect to these competencies (GAO, 2012b).

A third option may be to draw on competency assessments that are done within certain occupations. For example, the AW developed a competency model in which competencies were identified for broad levels (entry, journeyman, expert) within each career field using expert input. Employees and their supervisors then used an online assessment tool to perform a competency assessment. Although such competency data are likely to be available only for certain segments of the workforce, they may provide a starting point and a model for other competency data collection.

Military Data

There are a number of rich sources of data on military personnel and requirements, both at the DoD-wide level and at the service level.

Personnel Inventory

At the DoD-wide level, a number of files contain a rich set of information about active-duty and reserve-duty personnel. For example, the Active Duty Military Personnel Master File includes demographic characteristics, education and military training, occupation, pay grade, and ability ratings, while the Military Work Experience File (WEX) contains "transactions" that are generated whenever there are changes in an individual's key variables, such as service, pay grade, or occupation. Active- and reserve-duty pay files are also available for each of the services.

The Military Entrance Processing Command (MEPCOM) records the results of all tests given to incoming military recruits in the USMEPCOM Information Resource System (USMIRS). The database contains physical fitness scores, body weight, medical conditions, the Armed Services Vocational Aptitude Battery test, and vision tests. The individual services also maintain their own databases on accessions.

The services also collect a variety of information on promotions, assignments, duty, and other actions for DoD military service members through their individual databases. For example, MilPDS, MCFTS, and the Navy Standard Integrated Personnel System contain information about active, reserve, and retired personnel for the Air Force, Marines, and Navy, respectively.

Manpower Requirements and Authorizations

As with civilian data, there appears to be no centralized, DoD-wide system for military manpower data, but each service develops its own military manpower requirements as part of the planning process. As discussed above, the Air Force, Army, and the Navy maintain military authorizations in the MPES, SAMAS/FMS, and TFMMS databases, respectively.

Also like the civilian data, the military manpower requirements data feed into many applications and user interfaces. The Air Force's THRMIS system, which allows a comparison of personnel and manpower inventories and requirements, was discussed above. Similarly, the Army's Structure and Composition System allows managers to compare military personnel inventories against authorizations and assigns personnel to open spaces.

Competencies

Existing data related to military competencies are more readily available than data related to civilian competencies. On the personnel side, service-level databases track a variety of information, including language skills, academic performance, physical fitness, and performance reviews. On the manpower side, specific skill requirements are associated with positions in the MPES (Air Force) and TFMMS (Navy) manpower databases. These databases include Special Expertise Identifier (SEI) and Navy Enlisted Classification codes, respectively; they are more than simply occupation codes, and identify special skills, qualifications, and knowledge needed to meet the requirements of a position.

Contractor Data

To comply with NDAA FY 2010 requirements, OUSD (P&R) is required to plan for the appropriate mix of military, civilian, and contractor personnel and to identify the number of contractor full-time equivalents (FTEs). DoD has not historically accounted for contractors in terms of personnel, but rather in terms of costs, which are subsequently converted to contractor FTEs. Using the Federal Procurement Data System—Next Generation (FPDS-NG), a database that tracks contracting actions, contractor FTEs may be estimated by multiplying total contract obligations by the average ratio of direct labor dollars to total invoiced dollars for the particular contractor service and dividing by the average direct labor rate for the particular type of service (GAO, 2011a). In recent years, however, a number of efforts have been made to create an inventory of contractors.

Personnel Inventory

Beginning in 2005, the Army began collecting information on its contractor personnel through the Contractor Manpower Reporting Application (CMRA) (GAO, 2011a). Starting in FY 2013, OSD requires all DoD components, excluding the four intelligence agencies, to collect information using an enterprise-wide CMRA (eCMRA) (OSD, 2012). Contractor companies must enter the total involved amount, direct labor costs, and the direct labor hours (including subcontractor labor hours) for each contract into CMRA. The labor costs and labor hours are used to calculate the number of FTEs. eCMRA requires contractors to provide some details regarding work done, including the Federal Service Code and the unit identification code (UIC) and command "of the Requiring Activity that would be performing the mission if not for the contractor" (Contractor Manpower Reporting, undated). The data system is expected to be operational by FY 2014 and should include information on most contracts by FY 2016 (GAO, 2013).

Manpower Requirements and Authorizations

As discussed above, the Army's TAA process includes the identification of requirements for contractor personnel, and these requirements are available in TAADS and through FMSWeb, by UIC or occupation. However, the FMSWeb data do not always appear to be well-populated. The manpower databases of the other services do not appear to include contractor personnel requirements.

Competencies
The effort to collect contractor personnel inventories does not yet appear to include information about contractor competencies. Although eCMRA does require contractors to associate their work with a UIC and to provide several activity classifications, contractor hours are not separated by occupation.

A Closer Look at Manpower Systems: Case Study of the Air Force's Manning Programming and Execution System

In this section, we take a closer look at the Air Force's MPES for civilian and military employees. Although manpower data systems vary in their scope and structure, MPES illustrates some of the complexities involved in developing and maintaining manpower data, as well as the data elements that are included.

MPES is intended to record and display information about required billets needed to accomplish specific workloads, including the authorization status of the position. The system also allows the Air Force to identify deployable assets; build requests for additional manpower resources; adjust staffing levels at major commands (MAJCOMs), Wings, and Units across the world; assess current air and ground strength; and perform manpower reductions. The office of primary responsibility for MPES is AF/A1M (Air Force Directorate of Manpower, Organization, and Resources).

History
The data system that predated MPES was purchased from the U.S. Army and adapted to support intrinsically different requirements. This legacy system suffered from sluggish performance, frequent downtime, and the inability to fully support Air Force manpower requirements. Users often needed to shoehorn the Air Force data to fit Army manpower system-designed functionality through a time-consuming

process of reworking, tracking, and double-checking data to ensure that it was correct. MPES was launched in 2005 to modernize the Air Force's manpower data system. Segue Technologies, Inc., worked with AF/A1M to completely redesign the architecture, hardware, and software of MPES. After documenting the requirements for existing data and workflow, an efficient SQL server database was built, featuring a normalized data structure and a reliable archiving system with a complete offsite backup capability. The hardware footprint was increased from ten servers to more than 40. A new ColdFusion Web application accompanied the database. Segue continues to provide support for MPES on the Secret Internet Protocol Router Network (SIPRNet) and Nonsecure Internet Protocol Router Network (NIPRNet) (Segue Technologies, 2014).

Data Elements

Requirements in MPES for the current fiscal year and projected for the next five years are organized at the unit level, as defined by the personnel accounting symbol. There are more than 70 data elements that are used to define a requirement in MPES. The Air Force Specialty Code (AFSC) is a four- or five-character code used to identify a specific military occupation (e.g., Operations Intel Craftsman). The AFSC is similar to the Army and Marine's Military Occupation Specialty (MOS) system. For officers, the first two digits of the AFSC refer to the career field, the third digit is the functional area, and the fourth digit is the qualification level. Some positions also may have a prefix or suffix to designate more specific requirements or qualifications. For example, an 11H3 is a helicopter (H) pilot (11) with an intermediate skill level (3).

To complement the AFSC system by further identifying an activity and required experience set, military positions may also have an SEI, which is a three-character alphanumeric code that complements the AFSC. There are more than 1,000 possible SEIs offered by the Air Force that are awarded to airmen after they complete the qualification criteria. The first digit of the SEI identifies the activity, while the next two digits identify the experience set. Possible activities include acquisitions, computer systems, engineering, and health. An example of a qualification is electronic combat coordinator (EX), which is issued after completion of an electronic combat course and six years of flying experience. Managers can use SEIs to match open positions with qualified personnel. However, only 4 percent of positions in MPES include an SEI. The rate is higher for some career fields, such as development engineering, acquisition management, and intelligence, that have new occupations with evolving requirements. Civilians listed in MPES have an occupational series code in addition to an AFSC.

For military and civilian positions, MPES specifies whether the requirement was funded (authorized) or unfunded (not authorized). Contractor positions in MPES are in the form of contractor manpower equivalents (CMEs), which provides the Air Force with an estimate of the size of the contractor workforce. Because the responsibility of computing CMEs and updating MPES falls upon individual base-level servicing manpower offices and because Air Force Headquarters does not have much visibility into contractor activity at individual bases, AF/A1M faces a difficult task in trying to ensure accuracy of the CME figures. While military and civilian manpower authorizations in MPES must dovetail with the budget from Air Force Headquarters, CME figures in MPES do not have a direct impact on budget allocations. It is also unclear whether the CMEs are authorized or required. Thus, the incentive to keep contractor data accurate and up to date is less than the incentive to keep the military and civilian data up to date.

Many additional MPES elements serve administrative purposes (e.g., command identifier and name, organizational title and description, operating location). Other elements describe required attributes (e.g., grade, pay plan, military/civilian/contractor designation, functional category). Finally, there are several data elements related to required competencies, such as education, skills, and experience. The education level field in MPES designates whether an advanced degree is required for a position (and what that degree is). In some cases, a general area of study is recorded along within an advanced degree. Other variables designate language skills and cultural capabilities that are required for a position. For required languages, MPES includes a minimum speaking, listening, and reading score.

Determining Requirements for MPES

AFI 38-201 provides a detailed evaluation of the specific roles and responsibilities in determining the manpower requirements that are compiled in MPES. At the highest level, the process of determining military and civilian authorizations for MPES begins with Air Force Headquarters determining budget and resource allocations to the MAJCOMs. Within each MAJCOM, *manpower standards* are applied to generate the number of man-hours required at the unit level. Dividing the man-hours required by an appropriate manpower availability factor (MAF), which is defined as the average number of man-hours per month available for an individual to do primary duties, generates the number of FTEs a unit requires. At the end of this process, required positions are compiled, by unit, into Unit Manpower Documents (UMDs) within MPES. AF/A1M, with assistance from Air Force Functional Authority Mangers, is responsible for the Management Engineering Program (MEP) that creates the manpower standards, and it also updates MPES within 90 days of publication and reapplies manpower standards every two years, or earlier if dictated by significant workload or mission change. Manpower standards contain functional and organizational identifiers. Functional account codes group tasks that use similar equipment and processes, require related duties, or produce similar end products. Major functional groups include command, maintenance, operations, mission support, medical, research, and activities outside the Air Force. Organizational information is contained in organization structure codes. For example, the main elements of headquarters staff are manpower and personnel, intelligence, operations, logistics, plans and requirements, communications, installations and support, strategic plans and programs, analysis and assessments, and strategic deterrence (A1–A10). The Air Force Personnel Center (AFPC), in collaboration with each individual MAJCOM manpower staff, actually executes the MEP, calculating for the unit commanders their requirements (this was formerly the task of the Air Force Manpower Agency before it was inactivated and integrated into the AFPC in 2012).

AF/A1M is responsible for providing CME computation policy to individual base-level servicing manpower offices, which compute

CME and update MPES. The computation of CME varies depending on whether the contracts are competitive or noncompetitive. From a competitive contract, the CME is simply the most efficient organization FTE bid amount. Outside of competitive sourcing, the CME is derived from either an available FTE, a calculation from the MEP manpower standard, or directly from the budgeted contract value.

CHAPTER SIX

Key DoD Data Challenges and Opportunities

DoD is required to manage FCs and occupations. In this chapter, we discuss the key challenges to meeting this requirement, given currently available data systems. There are two dimensions to the challenges we identified. The first dimension involves the separate management of different types of data, while the second involves the lack of data that FC managers need to fulfill NDAA requirements.

Management of Different Data Systems

NDAA FY 2010 requires OUSD (P&R) to perform a gap analysis of the workforce. This requirement is difficult to fulfill in the current data environment. In most cases, personnel and manpower data are maintained separately. Although individual "faces" in the personnel data may be linked with information on the positions those individuals hold, the position data are not necessarily representative of the actual "spaces"—that is, the requirements or authorizations developed during the budgeting process. Our interviews also indicate that vacant positions for which local managers are hiring may not be identified in the centralized databases.

Managing workforces by occupation, at a centralized level, adds an additional layer of complexity. Centralized data systems, such as DCPDS (for civilians) and the Active Duty Military Personnel Master File (for military), contain information on occupation (OPM occupation codes for civilians and MOS or equivalent for military service members). FC managers are therefore able to track personnel stocks and flows for their occupations.

In contrast, manpower requirements are driven by organizations' need to support activities, rather than by occupations. For example, the Army's TAA process seeks to develop organizational models (Tables of Organization and Equipment, which serve as blueprints for operational units, as well as Tables of Distribution and Allowances for support units). Manpower datasets, which are maintained by individual services, reflect this focus. Although occupation codes may be available in the requirements or authorizations data, managers on the manpower side emphasize functions or activities, rather than occupations.

The differential focus of the personnel and manpower data systems on occupation versus activity is common to both military and civilian personnel. A second challenge related to data management is more relevant for civilians. Military manpower is centrally managed and is paid for out of a military personnel budget. In contrast, civilians and contractors are managed locally and are paid for out of other appropriations, such as the Operations and Maintenance (O&M) budget. A local command may choose to increase or decrease the number of civilians it hires by substituting funds from one part of the O&M budget to another. Our discussions suggest that commands are officially supposed to present the Civilian Human Resources Agency, which handles hiring, with a manpower document showing that the civilian position has been authorized prior to hiring a new civilian; in practice, however, this requirement does not appear to be enforced. Therefore, a local command may determine that it needs more civilian employees than were budgeted for during a service-level planning period. The command may choose to procure fewer services from contractors and to hire additional civilians. From the point of view of a command-level manager, the requirement for civilians has increased, and the number of on-board personnel has been increased to meet that requirement; therefore, there is no gap. The central on-board personnel file, DCPDS, will be updated to reflect the new on-board personnel. However, unless the central service-level manpower file is also updated to reflect the new requirement, a DoD-level manager will find that on-board personnel exceed requirements.

As we described in the previous chapter, the nature of personnel and manpower data poses challenges for workforce analyses at the occupation level within DoD. The challenges are even greater when it comes to analyzing workforce segments that cannot be easily identified by occupation codes. Important examples in DoD include the acquisition workforce, the expeditionary workforce, and the cyber workforce. With the exception of the acquisition workforce, there is no way to identify members of these other workforce segments in a systematic way, nor is it possible to obtain data on requirements information for these groups.

A Closer Look at Combining Personnel and Manpower Data: Case Study Using Army Data

In this section, we draw on two databases containing information about Army personnel to provide an example of how civilian personnel and manpower data might be compared. While each service and agency has its own data systems, and thus faces unique challenges in comparing personnel and manpower data, the Army systems illustrate some of the challenges that are likely to be faced in any effort that seeks to unite data maintained for different purposes. The personnel data we use come from DMDC and are thus similar to personnel data that would be available for all services and agencies. The manpower (requirements and authorizations) data are from the Army's FMSWeb system; in our research, the information in FMSWeb appears to be relatively comprehensive, relative to the manpower systems of other services and agencies within DoD.

We begin by comparing overall requirements, authorizations, and on-board civilian personnel counts. We then compare authorization and on-board personnel counts for the top ten Army commands and occupations. Our analysis shows a much larger discrepancy between the personnel and authorizations data at the occupation level than at the command level, highlighting the challenge of monitoring at the occupation level, particularly for narrowly defined MCOs. The fact that on-board personnel counts and authorization counts often differ by 10 percent or more, even at the Army command level, also illustrates the difficulty in determining whether these discrepancies are due to actual gaps or to changing requirements at local commands that are not reflected in the centralized manpower database.

Figure 6.1 shows that overall counts of requirements and authorizations for Army civilians follow a similar trend, with requirements always higher than authorizations, as we would expect. Personnel counts are consistently higher than authorized counts, and are sometimes higher than requirements. This situation is often referred to as an "overhire"—although, as discussed above, it is not clear whether the centrally maintained requirements and authorizations numbers reflect updated requirements from commands.

Similarly, Figure 6.2 shows the percentage by which on-board personnel exceed or fall short of authorizations for the ten largest Army commands (in terms of civilian personnel from DMDC) at the end of FY 2012. We do not include the Army Corps of Engineers in the figure, although it was the third largest command in terms of personnel at the end of FY 2012, because the personnel data indicate that

Figure 6.1
On-Board Personnel, Authorizations, and Requirements for Army Civilians

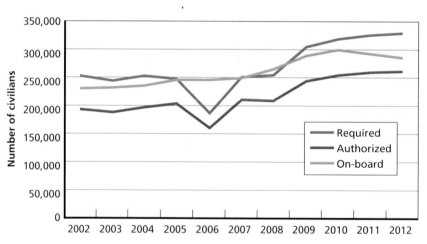

SOURCES: Authors' calculations based on requirements and authorizations data from FMSWeb and personnel data from DMDC.
NOTE: Number of required, authorized, and on-board Army civilians at the end of each FY from 2002 to 2012.
RAND RR543-6.1

Figure 6.2
Difference Between On-Board Personnel and Authorizations
for Army Civilians in the Largest Commands

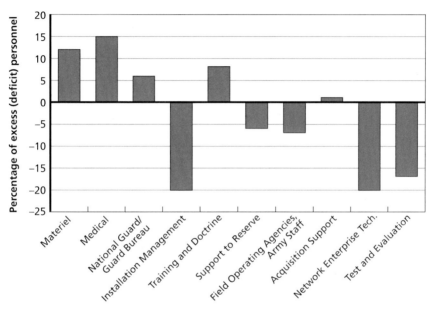

SOURCES: Authors' calculations based on requirements and authorizations data
from FMSWeb and personnel data from DMDC.
NOTE: Data are as of the end of FY 2012. The Army Corps of Engineers is excluded
for reasons discussed in the text. Percentage difference is calculated as number of
personnel minus number of authorizations, divided by number of authorizations.
RAND RR543-6.2

there are approximately 37,000 civilians, while there are only 10,000 authorizations. The reason for this large discrepancy is likely that the Corps is paid out of the Civil Works budget rather than the Defense budget.

Among the remaining commands, two (Materiel Command and Medical Command) exhibit personnel levels that are more than 10 percent above authorized levels, while another two (U.S. Army Installation Management Command [IMCOM] and U.S. Army Network Enterprise Technology Command [NETCOM]) exhibit personnel levels that are 20 percent below authorized levels.

At the occupation level, however, the discrepancies become more pronounced. Figure 6.3 shows the percentage by which on-board personnel exceed or fall short of authorizations for nine of the ten largest Army occupations (in terms of on-board personnel from DMDC) at the end of FY 2012. We exclude Civil Engineering because many of these personnel are associated with the Army Corps of Engineers, which is not comparable across the personnel and authorizations data.

On-board personnel exceed authorizations in all but one of these occupations. The extent of the gap varies substantially, ranging from

Figure 6.3
Difference Between On-Board Personnel and Authorizations for Army Civilians in the Largest Occupations by On-Board Personnel Counts

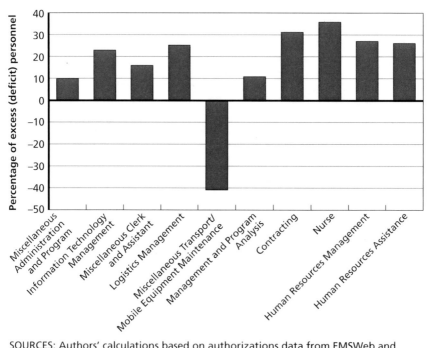

SOURCES: Authors' calculations based on authorizations data from FMSWeb and personnel data from DMDC.
NOTE: Data are as of the end of FY 2012. Civil Engineering is excluded for reasons discussed in the text. Percentage difference is calculated as number of personnel minus number of authorizations, divided by number of authorizations.
RAND RR543-6.3

a 10-percent discrepancy in the largest occupation (miscellaneous administration) to a 36-percent discrepancy for nurses. In the miscellaneous transportation occupation, personnel fall short of authorizations by 41 percent.

One potential reason for some of these discrepancies is that authorizations are allocated to broad occupational categories, whereas personnel are hired into specific occupations. Figure 6.4 illustrates this issue by showing the percentage by which personnel exceed or fall short of authorizations in the *largest occupations as defined by authorization*

Figure 6.4
Difference Between On-Board Personnel and Authorizations for Army Civilians in the Largest Occupations by Authorization Counts

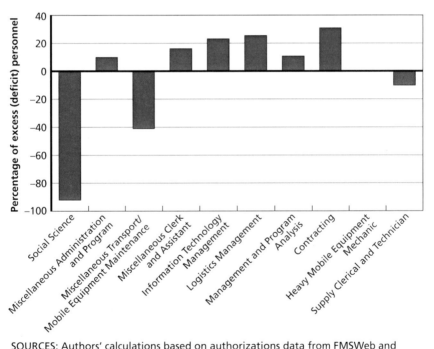

SOURCES: Authors' calculations based on authorizations data from FMSWeb and personnel data from DMDC.
NOTE: Data are as of end of FY 2012. Percentage difference is calculated as the number of personnel minus the number of authorizations, divided by the number of authorizations.
RAND RR543-6.4

rather than personnel counts. In this case, the single largest occupation is "0101," which is described as "Social Science" and has more than 17,000 authorizations. However, there were only 1,400 on-board personnel with this occupation code at the end of FY 2012, according to DMDC data. Similarly, "Miscellaneous Transportation/Mobile Equipment Maintenance" has nearly 14,000 authorizations but only 8,000 on-board personnel. It is possible that the reason for the discrepancy is that the 0101 code for Social Science and the 5801 code for Miscellaneous Transportation may be catchall categories in the authorizations database.

We examine this possibility in Figure 6.5, where we analyze personnel and authorizations by broader occupation groups or families, as defined by OPM; for example, the General Administrative, Clerical, and Office Services Group includes all occupational series from 0301 to 0399. This grouping reduces the discrepancies to some extent, but challenges remain. The Social Science occupation series (0101) showed 90 percent fewer personnel (1,400) than authorizations (17,000). The broader Social Science, Psychology, and Welfare Group (0100) still shows 60 percent fewer personnel (8,500) than authorizations (22,500). Similarly, the discrepancy in the Miscellaneous Transportation series (5801) remains in the broader Transportation/Mobile Equipment Family (5800), which has 31 percent fewer personnel (14,000) than authorizations (20,000).

Data Availability

The issues discussed above make it challenging to conduct a gap analysis for civilian personnel, particularly at the function or occupation level. Nonetheless, data on military and civilian personnel and authorization counts are available, allowing managers to conduct some type of analysis.

A more challenging issue is the lack of availability of data for the contractor workforce. The contractor workforce can be divided into on-site and off-site contractors, and a separate set of challenges applies to each group. With respect to on-site contractors, the Army does include

Figure 6.5
Difference Between On-Board Personnel and Authorizations for Army Civilians in the Largest Occupations by Authorization Counts, Broad Occupation Groups

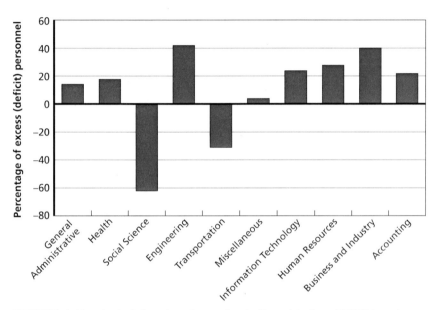

SOURCES: Authors' calculations based on authorizations data from FMSWeb and personnel data from DMDC.
NOTE: Data are as of end of FY 2012. Percentage difference is calculated as the number of personnel minus the number of authorizations, divided by the number of authorizations.
RAND RR543-6.5

requirements and authorizations for certain contractors in FMSWeb (Figure 6.6).

Nonetheless, there are several key limitations. First, our analysis of these requirements, as well as our discussions with various data users, suggest that they are not well-populated and may not be frequently updated. This is particularly true with respect to occupational data. Figure 6.7 shows authorizations and requirements for Army contractors for the ten largest occupations. More than one-third of the occupational data are missing, while another 25 percent of contractors are classified under OPM code 0301, "Miscellaneous Administration

Figure 6.6
Authorizations and Requirements for Army Contractors by Command: Ten Largest Commands by Authorizations

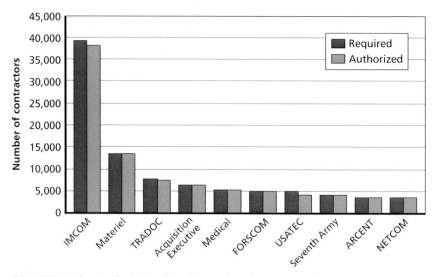

SOURCES: Authors' calculations based on authorizations data from FMSWeb and personnel data from DMDC.
NOTES: Number of authorized and required Army contractors in the ten largest commands (in terms of number of contractor authorizations) at the end of FY 2012. ARCENT = U.S. Army Central, USATEC = U.S. Army Test and Evaluation Command, FORSCOM = U.S. Army Forces Command, TRADOC = U.S. Army Training and Doctrine Command.
RAND RR543-6.6

and Program." Thus, it is difficult for FC managers to determine the functions of approximately two-thirds of the contractor workforce.

Another limitation of the contractor data involves its scope. Our interviews indicated that contractor data in FMSWeb are limited to positions that are expected to exist in two years. Therefore, contractors under programs such as the Logistics Civil Augmentation Program (LOGCAP) may not appear in FMSWeb.

Finally, if contractor data were more widely collected at a central level, the same challenge that applies to civilian data—namely, that local changes in the number of contractor requirements are not updated in the centralized requirements—would also apply.

Figure 6.7
Authorizations and Requirements for Army Contractors by Occupation: Ten Largest Occupations by Authorizations

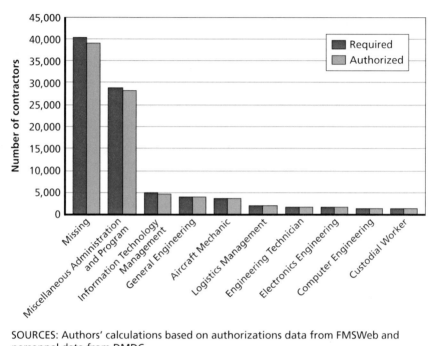

SOURCES: Authors' calculations based on authorizations data from FMSWeb and personnel data from DMDC.
NOTE: Number of authorized and required Army contractors in the ten largest occupations (in terms of number of contractor authorizations) at the end of FY 2012.
RAND RR543-6.7

For offsite contractors, the Army has been collecting data on contractor FTEs using the CMRA tool. The DoD-wide rollout of eCMRA should help to produce overall FTEs for offsite contractors; however, contractors are not required to identify FTEs by occupation. Thus, even after eCMRA is widely adopted by DoD contractors, FC managers will not be able to use CMRA data to infer the count of offsite contractors in their occupations. We also note that in the absence of directly collected contractor data, various DoD agencies have been estimating contractor FTEs based on contract value from FPDS-NG combined with estimates of the share of contract spent on labor, as well as labor costs (GAO, 2011a, 2013).

Finally, data collection on competencies is in its infancy. Competency models have been developed for many MCOs, and the Competency Assessment Tool may be more widely used going forward. However, even if competency assessments are performed routinely, managing competency gaps is still likely to prove challenging.

Box 6.1: Workforce Planning at NASA

We spoke with workforce mangers at NASA, which has some experience with both contractor and competency data collection and management at a centralized level. We provide a brief summary of their experience, which highlights some of the challenges involved.

NASA manages a workforce of 19,000 employees, who are distributed across nine centers around the country. Planning takes place at the agency level as well as within each center and includes civilians as well as on-site contractors. Off-site contractors are excluded from workforce planning, as NASA requires specific deliverables from off-site contractors, rather than specific personnel.

At the agency-wide level, NASA's workforce management focuses on levels rather than competencies. The goal is not to change supply to meet an assigned demand, but rather to allow flexibility in either supply or demand to create an appropriate match. This is to some extent driven by NASA's culture of semi-independent field centers, which have associated personnel and which may be focused on specific functions. In the longer term, workforce planners can shape the size of the workforce; in the shorter term, they focus on shaping the portfolio of work at each center. A key tool that managers use is project-level time tracking by employees. By tracking the time that individual employees spend working on projects, workforce planners can better identify gaps between project needs (demand) and individual availability (supply).

Many short-term workforce decisions are made at the center level. Centers are given FTE budgets for civilians and work-year equivalent (WYE) budgets for on-site contractors, based on their missions. Individual centers use a variety of different processes and tools for assigning and tracking work. Although decisions about

Box 6.1—continued

hiring off-site contractors are made at a programmatic level, individual centers have some flexibility in terms of how much money they spend on contractors versus other procurement, such as travel or supplies.

In response to a specific, historical challenge, NASA created a competency management system at the agency level. This system included a way to track personnel competencies, as well as competency requirements for each position. Personnel are assigned NASA Class Codes, which are analogous to competencies, and NASA has reported some data to OPM based on these codes. Although workforce planners do have the ability to access competency data, they identified several challenges associated with competency management at the agency level. First, defining competencies was challenging, as each center might interpret a competency requirement differently. In addition, rolling up information to the agency level proved difficult. Finally, workforce managers noted that critical qualitative information, such as an individual employee's ability to move across positions with different competency requirements, would not be captured by a database.

Today, NASA still maintains its competency-related data systems but no longer uses them for agency-level planning. Rather, the agency is moving toward more agile methods of managing the workforce. Most competency gap analysis takes place at the center level, where managers have a good understanding of their current workforce and can incorporate qualitative information into their decisions. At the agency level, workforce planners send out data calls to centers at a variety of times. These calls allow them to factor in qualitative considerations that would not be feasible in a global approach. In addition, they can question centers about mismatches between supply and demand. Since centers incur the full costs of their employees and are primarily responsible for matching supply with demand, the large centers have built up a substantial capacity to do workforce planning, including their own specific tools.

Box 6.1—continued

The NASA example highlights the potential difficulties that even a sophisticated data management system faces with respect to contractor data and competencies. NASA centers have some of the same flexibility in terms of how many contractors to hire, as do commands and other local offices within DoD. Therefore, NASA includes requests for contractor WYE in its periodic data calls to centers. However, they only track on-site contractors, not off-site contractors. Moreover, contractor data are not kept in the personnel data systems. After trying a more centralized management approach, most competency management is now done at a decentralized level, with some aggregation through periodic data calls.

CHAPTER SEVEN

Conclusions and Recommendations

The FY 2010 NDAA requires DoD to periodically submit to Congress a strategic plan for the DoD-wide civilian workforce that, among other things, assesses gaps in the current and projected civilian workforce, as well as the appropriate mix of military, civilian, and contractor capabilities within mission-critical occupations. This report describes numerous approaches and specific tools that are available to help managers analyze the workforce in support of workforce planning. Each of the approaches and tools we reviewed has strengths and weaknesses. The best tool or approach will depend on the question that needs to be addressed and the resources (data and expertise) available. The relative costs and benefits of different workforce analysis techniques vary based on the level at which they are applied. In assessing the costs and benefits of using a particular tool or approach, it is important to recognize that workforce analysis requires resources. Two types of resources are worth highlighting: (1) the time and resources required to collect and maintain data for workforce analysis and (2) the capacity to analyze the data and use the analysis to inform decisions. A key question is whether the resources are available at the level at which DoD seeks to conduct workforce planning and analysis.

DoD Data Limitations May Impede Total Workforce Analysis of Functional Communities and Occupations

The report also summarizes the data sources available in DoD to support total workforce analysis at the occupation level. Our review suggests that the existing data sources may impede such analysis. Ideally, DoD workforce managers would have access to a centralized database that contains military, civilian, and contractor personnel and manpower data from all DoD services and agencies; that links personnel and manpower data; and that identifies the occupation or function associated with each individual and each position. The DCPDS, Active Duty Military Personnel Master File, and WEX data systems are rich sources of centralized data for on-board personnel, but attempts to centralize other aspects of manpower and personnel data have not been similarly successful. Moreover, options for linking manpower and workforce data—especially to analyze functional communities or occupations—are highly limited. Systematic data collection on contractor manpower and personnel and on personnel competencies and competency requirements is in its infancy.

Options for Improving Data Systems Involve Trade-Offs

Developing data reporting requirements, and modifying existing data systems, to address the data limitations we identified will require substantial time and effort. Past experience with the development of DoD-wide systems and reporting requirements suggests that new requirements are likely to experience resistance and the quality of data collected may be lower than expected. As such, we provide an array of options for conducting workforce analysis at the functional community or occupation level, ranging from short-term options that can be implemented with existing data and analytic capabilities to long-term options that would require substantial retooling of data systems and processes.

Short-Term Options

In the short term, DoD should consider options for supporting occupation-level analyses that are based on existing data systems and tools.

DoD maintains rich personnel databases for military personnel and civilians. This report discusses several models that already draw on these databases to analyze workforce supply at a DoD-wide level. Compiling demand information for DoD poses greater challenges. Individual services and agencies spend significant resources to model their workforce requirements—particularly in terms of military personnel—during the budgeting process. These efforts result in requirements and authorizations data that can be used by DoD workforce planners. For example, if the authorizations data are treated as targets, then DoD workforce planners can use one of many existing supply projection models, coupled with existing personnel data, to identify hiring rates that would be required to meet those targets. The RAND Inventory Model provides foundational support to the Defense Civilian Personnel Advisory Service, Strategic Human Capital Planning Division (DCPAS-SHCPD), to perform this type of exercise.

This method is not without its challenges. The budgeting process is focused on activities rather than occupations. Although managers are asked to report requirements by occupation, in setting targets, they are likely to put more effort into specifying totals for an activity, with an understanding that that there may be some flexibility to reallocate requirements across occupations or across categories of personnel (especially civilian and contractor). An apparent gap between the authorizations and on-board personnel data at the occupation level may reflect such substitutions. The challenges are magnified when considering personnel gaps for contractors because occupational data are often missing in the authorizations data, and personnel data collection on contractors is in its infancy.

Nonetheless, comparing head counts of military and civilian employees can shed light on which occupations appear to face the most substantial gaps between supply and demand. Moreover, examining changes in those gaps over time—or in the military/civilian mix of an occupational workforce—may be informative.

Finally, we note that competency data are still extremely limited, although ongoing efforts are in progress to systematically collect competency information. To the extent that competency requirements include factors that can be observed in the personnel data—such as education, training, or language proficiency—DoD workforce managers can perform preliminary assessments.

Another short-term option is for local managers to proceed with new or ongoing data collection efforts targeting their workforces. For example, even targeted or nonsystematic exit surveys that explore the reasons behind separation could be helpful in understanding why employees in critical occupations depart. Similarly, targeted collection of competency information could be used by managers at a local level, even if there is limited capacity in the short term to roll up the data.

Medium-Term Options
As the availability of systematic data on workforce competencies and the contractor workforce improves over time, additional workforce analyses will become feasible. Over the next several years, contractor personnel data are likely to become more available, as eCMRA is implemented throughout DoD. Therefore, DoD workforce managers may soon be able to compare contractor authorizations from the budgeting process with contractor FTEs. To conduct this analysis at the occupation level, it may be necessary to modify eCMRA data collection to include a breakdown of contactor FTEs by occupation.

DoD has also made substantial efforts to improve collection of competency data. If quantitative competency assessment data become available, DoD workforce managers may be able to compare personnel competencies against competency requirements. Such quantitative measures may be fairly easy to aggregate across DoD for the purposes of a DoD-wide analysis. What remains unclear at this time, however, is whether the quality of data on personnel and position competencies will be high and the data will be well-populated. It may be difficult to ensure that managers perform the assessments as required. Different managers may interpret the competency rankings in different ways, or rankings may become subject to challenges that have plagued rating systems, such as bunching in the top ratings.

An alternative to analyses that rely on systematic DoD-wide personnel and requirements data would be a limited, bottom-up analysis focused on high-priority MCOs or functional areas. Bottom-up analyses can be time-consuming and potentially costly but may be better able to capture qualitative insights from local managers. A survey tool could be used to identify gaps among civilian, military, and contractor employees performing high-priority functions. These reported gaps could be aggregated across activities.

Aggregating this sort of qualitative data would be more challenging than aggregating quantitative data. Instead of quantifying the number by which demand exceeds supply (or supply exceeds demand), a DoD functional manager might note that 30 out of 40 managers identified a lack of employees with a particular skill, thus signaling a broad need. Another advantage is that the survey could probe to find out whether the manager would prefer a different occupational mix or competency mix. Although such survey data are imprecise, they can provide insights into a key limitation of workforce modeling based on historical quantitative data. One of the main challenges with quantitative workforce modeling is that historical data reflect both supply and demand conditions. If a manager has a contractor-heavy workforce, it may not reflect a preference for contractors, but rather an inability to find sufficient civilians with the right skill set. When surveying managers about current workforce gaps, workforce analysts could elicit manager judgments about future workload and personnel demand at the same time.

Such targeted, qualitative surveys may be particularly useful in the context of cross-cutting workforces, such as the cyber or expeditionary workforces that cannot be easily identified in the personnel or requirements data using occupation codes or other data codes. Qualitative surveys of local managers could identify employees across occupational groups who work in these cross-cutting areas. Managers would also be able to articulate specific gaps and challenges they see in managing these workforces.

For example, human capital management of the cyber workforce is a high-priority interest but is still in the process of taking shape. As a consequence, it is difficult to use existing data structures to distinguish cyber workers. Often, cyber positions draw on traditional occupations (such as information technologies, computer engineering, and electronics engineering) but then also require very specific competencies (e.g., network mapping and exploitation, familiarity with NSA tool sets, management of network attack systems, telecommunications knowledge). In the longer run, the federal government should consider whether new occupation codes should be developed to capture this expertise and distinguish it from the more traditional but related occupations. In the meantime, surveys may be a useful approach to identifying and understanding workforce gaps. Potential survey questions that might be asked of a functional manager for analysis of the cyber workforce include the following:

- **Supply-side questions**
  - Identify the number and skills of personnel under your supervision who would be designated as part of the cyber workforce.
  - How are they distributed across military, civilian, and contractor personnel?
- **Demand-side questions**
  - What skills and competencies are required to meet your organization's cyber objectives, and how should they be distributed across grade and specialty?
  - What training, education, and experience are needed to fulfill your organization's cyber objectives?
  - What metric do you use to quantify your organization's current cyber-related workload, and how do you see this changing in the future? How does this translate to the number of personnel required in the future?
  - How do you see demand for specific cyber-related competencies changing in the future?
- **Gap analysis and solutions questions**
  - Is your group able to meet its objective, in terms of cyber operations, with the current workforce? If not, what needs to be done in terms of hiring new staff and training existing staff?
  - Ideally, how would you adjust current personnel (in terms of number and competencies) to meet the current demand for cyber work?
  - How would you adjust the mixture of military, civilian, and contractor workers?
  - Are there ways to make the utilization of cyber personnel more efficient in your organization?

Long-Term Options

These options are presented less as forecasts of the types of analysis that will be common in the future and more as aspirational goals for top-down and bottom-up analysis over the long run. In other words, we represent them as not as options that *will* be possible but options that *can* be possible. In describing these options, we discuss what additional data and support would be needed to achieve the "gold standard" of supply and demand analysis.

An ideal top-down analysis of manpower gaps would require information about supply and demand that could be appropriately linked by either function or occupation. In Chapter Six, we performed a case study of a small subset of the workforce, Army civilians, for which we were able to obtain matching supply and demand data. Each component within DoD operates its own requirements database, which makes the task of generalizing our analysis much more difficult. To fully implement a DoD-wide top-down analysis would require a substantial investment in data collection—most notably collecting supply information for contractors by occupation and occupational/functional information for demand requirements of military, civilian, and contractor employees. Furthermore, the ability to perform gap analysis hinges on the ability to align supply data with demand data, which requires cooperation from every participant in the data-generating process to ensure standardization and compatibility.

The scope and the potential expense of such an ambitious data collection are daunting, and several notable barriers challenge the potential viability of a gold standard top-down analysis. A logistical challenge is creating an incentive for managers to report information regularly and completely. For example, one option for tracking and analyzing specialized workforces such as the cyber workforce would be to develop a reporting requirement for managers to identify these segments of the workforce and report personnel and authorization information on them to DCPDS, similar to how the acquisition workforce is tracked. Such a requirement would impose a significant data collection burden on local managers, who might resist implementation. A systematic reporting requirement is enduring and makes the most sense where DoD anticipates a long-term need to track the subsegment of the workforce. The acquisition workforce is currently required to do so, but even there, the data available on requirements are often incomplete. Across a heterogeneous organization such as DoD, managers may be reluctant to provide broad visibility into their own personnel management decisions. A solution could be reached through implementation of a new IT system that updates the central data system in real time with information about employee movement and about requirements and authorizations pulled automatically from the units.

A more fundamental challenge relates to the idea that databases mainly track characteristics and designators that are currently of interest (not what will be of interest in the future). It is very difficult to anticipate future data needs. In such a way, data collection occurs reactively—by the time new designators are desired, the opportunity to collect historical data on these designators has passed. Thus, new data fields may be added, but without periodic and often-costly reorganizations of data structures, this contributes to data bloat. Overreliance on top-down analysis also has the potential to overlook valuable qualitative insights (e.g., certain employees are more fungible from one competency to another). These challenges may be particularly salient if, as some workforce planners suggest, tracking individual competencies becomes less important than gauging organizational capabilities. Capabilities are defined by Ulrich (2013) as "what the organization is known for, what it is good at doing, and how it patterns activities to deliver value." This potential direction in workforce management suggests that the characteristics that managers will want to track in the future may be very different from those that are tracked today and may also be harder to quantify and record in a centralized database.

An alternative and potentially more feasible recommendation for the long term would be to build capacity for workforce analysis at the "local" level. Just as with specialized qualitative questionnaires for high-interest groups in the medium term, in the long term more standardized qualitative questions may be rolled out to all local offices/commands concerning what gaps exist. The determination of what constitutes the "local" level depends on the locus at which dollar budgets are allocated and reshuffled across specific positions. For example, in the Air Force, the MAJCOMs serve as the local level, or the business unit level, determining the number of contractors and civilians to hire. Furthermore, it would be worthwhile for OPM to work with other offices in DoD in arriving at more productive levels of analysis, rather than occupation. More flexibility can be achieved by keeping functions more general than a specific MCO.

In making this recommendation, our point is not that occupations or functional communities should not be analyzed at the DoD-wide level. However, given the challenges with requirements data, it may be more effective to compare supply and demand at a local level and then to aggregate the information about gaps to the DoD-wide level to present an overall picture of workforce health in a particular occupation. Performing an initial analysis using the central manpower systems, and using data calls when needed to investigate potentially large or growing gaps, would help to balance the need to collect information against the goal of minimizing reporting requirements.

References

Angus, Derek C., Mark A. Kelley, Robert J. Schmitz, Alan White, and John Popovich, "Current and Projected Workforce Requirements for Care of the Critically Ill and Patients with Pulmonary Disease," *Journal of the American Medical Association*, Vol. 284, No. 21, 2000, pp. 2762–2770.

Asch, Beth J., James R. Hosek, and John T. Warner, "New Economics of Manpower in the Post-Cold War Era," in Keith Hartley and Todd Sandler, eds., *Handbook of Defense Economics*, Vol. 2, No. 1, Amsterdam: Elsevier, 2007.

Atwater, D. M., J. A. Nelson, and R. J. Niehaus, "Building Local Labor Market Dynamics into Workforce 2000," in R. J. Niehaus and K. F. Price, eds., *Bottom Line Results from Strategic Human Resource Planning*, New York: Plenum Press, 1991, pp. 23–39.

Australian Public Service Commission, *Australian Public Service Workforce Planning Guide: Supply Analysis*, 2011.

Australian Public Service Commission, *Australian Public Service Strategic Workforce and Analysis Reporting Guide*, 2012.

Bartholomew, David J., and Andrew F. Forbes, *Statistical Techniques for Manpower Planning*, Chichester: John Wiley & Sons, 1979.

Basu, S., and R. Schroeder, "Incorporating Judgments in Sales Forecasts: Application of the Delphi Method at American Hoist & Derrick," *Interfaces*, Vol. 7, No. 3, 1977, pp. 18–27.

Bechet, Thomas, "Breathing New Life into Old Techniques," in Dan Ward, Thomas P. Bechet, and Robert Tripp, eds., *Human Resource Forecasting and Modeling*, New York: The Human Resource Planning Society, 1994.

Bechet, Thomas, *Strategic Staffing*, New York: AMACOM, 2008.

Bechet, Thomas, and William Maki, "Modeling and Forecasting: Focusing on People as a Strategic Resource," *Human Resource Planning*, Vol. 10, No. 4, 1987, pp. 209–218.

Better, Marco, Fred Glover, Dave Sutherland, and Manual Laguna, "SWP: A Rigorous Simulation Optimization Approach," in Dan L. Ward, Rob Tripp, and Bill Maki, eds., *Positioned: Strategic Workforce Planning That Gets the Right Person in the Right Job*, New York: AMACOM, 2013.

Black, D., "Measuring Relative Productivity and Staffing Levels in a Federal Procurement Office," *Journal of Supply Chain Management*, Vol. 31, No. 3, 1995, p. 44.

Bulmash, Julie, Nita Chhinzer, and Elizabeth Speers, *Strategic Planning for Human Resources*, Whitby, Ontario, Canada: McGraw Hill-Ryerson Higher Education, 2010.

Camm, Frank, Karin E. Kitchens, Peter Lewis, and Wade M. Markel, "How External Demands Affect the Size and Structure of the Army Generating Force," unpublished RAND Corporation research, 2011.

Centers for Disease Control and Prevention, "Gaining Consensus Among Stakeholders Through the Nominal Group Technique," *Evaluation Briefs*, No. 7, November 2006. As of February 25, 2013: www.cdc.gov/healthyyouth/evaluation/pdf/brief7.pdf

Chan, Edward W., Nancy Y. Moore, and Mary E. Chenoweth, "A Scorecard for Evaluating Contracting Staffing and Procurement Administrative Lead Time Models," unpublished RAND Corporation research, 2012.

Clark, David, "Navy Officer Manpower Optimization Incorporating Budgetary Constraints," Thesis in Operations Research, Monterey, Calif.: Naval Postgraduate School, 2009.

Collins, Roger W., Saul I. Gass, and Edward E. Rosendahl, "The ASCAR Model for Evaluating Military Manpower Policy," *Interfaces*, Vol. 13, No. 3, 1983, pp. 44–53.

Contractor Manpower Reporting, *Contractor Manpower Reporting Application, Version 3.6, Full User Guide*, undated. As of May 19, 2014: https://cmra.army.mil/Help/Full_User_Guide.pdf

Cooper, Richard A., Thomas E. Getzen, Heather J. McKee, and Prakash Laud, "Economic and Demographic Trends Signal an Impending Physician Shortage," *Health Affairs*, Vol. 21, No. 1, 2002, pp. 140–154.

Dalal, S., D. Khodyakov, R. Srinivasan, S. Straus, and J. Adams, "ExpertLens: A System for Eliciting Opinions from a Large Pool of Non-Collocated Experts with Diverse Knowledge," *Technological Forecasting and Social Change*, Vol. 78, No. 8, 2011, pp. 1426–1444.

Dalkey, Norman Crolee, and Olaf Helmer-Hirschberg, *An Experimental Application of the Delphi Method to the Use of Experts*, Santa Monica, Calif.: RAND Corporation, RM-727/1, 1962. As of May 16, 2014: http://www.rand.org/pubs/research_memoranda/RM727z1.html

Delbecq, Andre L., and Andrew H. Van de Ven, "A Group Process Model for Problem Identification and Program Planning," *Journal of Applied Behavioral Science*, Vol. 7, 1971, pp. 466–492.

Dill, Michael J., and Edward S. Salsberg, *The Complexities of Physician Supply and Demand: Projections Through 2025*, Washington, D.C.: Association of American Medical Colleges, Center for Workforce Studies, 2008.

DoD—*see* U.S. Department of Defense.

Edwards, John F., "A Survey of Manpower Planning Models and Their Application," *Journal of the Operational Research Society*, Vol. 34, No. 11, 1983, pp. 1031–1040.

Emmerichs, Robert M., Cheryl Y. Marcum, and Albert A. Robbert, *An Operational Process for Workforce Planning*, Santa Monica, Calif.: RAND Corporation, MR-1684/1-OSD, 2004. As of May 16, 2014: http://www.rand.org/pubs/monograph_reports/MR1684z1.html

Feuer, Michael, "From Environmental Scanning to Human Resource Planning: A Linkage Model Applied to Universities," *Human Resource Planning*, Vol. 6, No. 2, 1983, pp. 69–83.

GAO—*see* U.S. Government Accountability Office.

Gass, Saul I., "A Process for Determining Priorities and Weights for Large-Scale Linear Goal Programmes," *Journal of the Operational Research Society*, Vol. 37, No. 8, 1986, pp. 779–785.

Gates, Susan M., Christine Eibner, and Edward G. Keating, *Civilian Workforce Planning in the Department of Defense: Different Levels, Different Roles*, Santa Monica, Calif.: RAND Corporation, MG-449-OSD, 2006. As of May 16, 2014: http://www.rand.org/pubs/monographs/MG449.html

Gates, Susan M., Edward G. Keating, Bryan Tysinger, Adria D. Jewell, Lindsay Daugherty, and Ralph Masi, *The Defense Acquisition Workforce: An Analysis of Personnel Trends Relevant to Policy, 1993–2006*, Santa Monica, Calif.: RAND Corporation, TR-572-OSD, 2008. As of May 16, 2014: http://www.rand.org/pubs/technical_reports/TR572.html

Gates, Susan M., Edward G. Keating, Bryan Tysinger, Adria D. Jewell, Lindsay Daugherty, and Ralph Masi, *The Department of the Navy's Civilian Acquisition Workforce: An Analysis of Recent Trends*, Santa Monica, Calif.: RAND Corporation, TR-555-NAVY, 2009. As of May 16, 2014: http://www.rand.org/pubs/technical_reports/TR555.html

Gates, Susan M., Beth Roth, Sinduja Srinivasan, and Lindsay Daugherty, *Analyses of the Department of Defense Acquisition Workforce: Update to Methods and Results Through FY 2011*, Santa Monica, CA: RAND Corporation, RR-110-OSD, 2013. As of May 16, 2014: http://www.rand.org/pubs/research_reports/RR110.html

Gatewood, R. D., and E. J. Gatewood, "The Use of Expert Data in Human Resource Planning: Guidelines from Strategic Forecasting," *Human Resource Planning*, Vol. 6, No. 2, 1983, pp. 83–94.

Greene, William H., *Econometric Analysis*, New York: Prentice Hall, 2003.

Helmer, O., "Problems in Futures Research: Delphi and Causal Cross-Impact Analysis," *Futures*, February 1977, pp. 2–31.

Hinrichs, John R., and Robert F. Morrison, "Human Resource Planning in Support of Research and Development," *Human Resource Planning*, Vol. 3, No. 4, 1980, pp. 201–210.

Holz, Betty W., and James M. Wroth, "Improving Strength Forecasts: Support for Army Manpower Management," *Interfaces*, Vol. 10, No. 6, 1980, pp. 37–52.

Joyce, Catherine M., John J. McNeil, and Johannes U. Stoelwinder, "More Doctors, but Not Enough: Australian Medical Workforce Supply, 2001–2012," *MJA*, Vol. 184, No. 9, 2006, pp. 441–446.

Kirkwood, Craig W., "Systems Dynamics Models: A Quick Introduction," last updated January 12, 2013. As of May 19, 2014:
http://www.public.asu.edu/~kirkwood/sysdyn/SDIntro/SDIntro.htm

Lee, Paul P., Catherine A. Jackson, and Daniel A. Relles, *Estimating Eye Care Provider Supply and Workforce Requirements*, Santa Monica, Calif.: RAND Corporation, MR-516-AAO, 1995. As of May 16, 2014:
http://www.rand.org/pubs/monograph_reports/MR516.html

Lempert, R. J., S. W. Popper and S. C. Bankes, *Shaping the Next One Hundred Years: New Methods for Quantitative, Long-Term Policy Analysis*, Santa Monica, Calif.: RAND Corporation, MR-1626-RPC, 2003. As of May 16, 2014:
http://www.rand.org/pubs/monograph_reports/MR1626.html

Linard, Keith, *System Dynamics Modeling: HR Planning and Maintenance of Corporate Knowledge*, New South Wales, Australia: University of New South Wales, 2003.

Lomas, Jonathan, Greg L. Stoddart, and Morris L. Barer, "Supply Projections as Planning: A Critical Review of Forecasting Net Physician Requirements in Canada," *Social Science Medicine*, Vol. 20, No. 4, 1985, pp. 411–424.

Makridakis, S., and Wheelwright, S. C., *Forecasting: Methods and Applications*, New York: Wiley, 1978.

Manganaris, Alex, "The Evolution of Strategic Workforce Planning Within Government Agencies," in Dan L. Ward, Rob Tripp, and Bill Maki, eds., *Positioned: Strategic Workforce Planning That Gets the Right Person in the Right Job*, New York: AMACOM, 2013.

Masi, Ralph, Anny Wong, John E. Boon, Jr., Peter Schirmer, and Jerry M. Sollinger, *Supporting the U.S. Army Human Resources Command's Human Capital Strategic Planning*, Santa Monica, Calif.: RAND Corporation, MG-828-A, 2009. As of May 16, 2014:
http://www.rand.org/pubs/monographs/MG828.html

Mattock, Michael G., James Hosek, and Beth J. Asch, *Reserve Participation and Cost Under a New Approach to Reserve Compensation*, Santa Monica, Calif.: RAND Corporation, MG-1153-OSD, 2012. As of May 16, 2014:
http://www.rand.org/pubs/monographs/MG1153.html

Meehan, R. H., and S. B. Ahmed, "Forecasting Human Resources Requirements: A Demand Model," *Human Resource Planning*, Vol. 13, No. 4, 1990, pp. 297–307.

Milkovich, G. T., A. J. Annoni, and T. A. Mahoney, "The Use of the Delphi Procedures in Manpower Forecasting," *Management Science*, Vol. 19, No. 4, 1972, pp. 381–388.

NASA—*see* National Aeronautics and Space Administration.

Nataraj, Shanthi, Lawrence M. Hanser, Frank Camm, and Jessica Yeats, *The Future of the Army's Civilian Workforce: Comparing Projected Inventory with Anticipated Requirements and Estimating Cost Under Different Personnel Policies*, Santa Monica, Calif.: RAND Corporation, RR-576, 2014. As of September 12, 2014:
http://www.rand.org/pubs/research_reports/RR576.html

National Aeronautics and Space Administration, *NASA Workforce Planning Desk Guide, Version 2*, 2008.

Niehaus, Richard, "Human Resource Planning Flow Models," *Human Resource Planning*, Vol. 3, No. 4, 1980, pp. 87–97.

Niehaus, Richard, "Models for Human Resource Decisions," *Human Resource Planning*, Vol. 2, No. 4, 1988, pp. 95–107.

O'Brien-Pallas, Linda, Andrea Baumann, Gail Donner, Gail Tomblin, Jacquelyn Lochhaas-Gerlach, and Marcia Luba, "Forecasting Models for Human Resources in Health Care," *Journal of Advanced Nursing*, Vol. 33, No. 1, 2001, pp. 120–129.

Office of the Secretary of Defense, Memorandum, "Enterprise-Wide Contractor Manpower Reporting Application," November 12, 2012.

OPM—*see* U.S. Office of Personnel Management.

Pinfield, Lawrence T., "A Case Study of the Application of a Terminations Forecast Model," *Human Resource Planning*, Vol. 4, No. 2, 1981, pp. 18–32.

Pinfield, Lawrence T., and Steven L. McShane, "Applications of Manpower Planning in Two School Districts," *Human Resource Planning*, Vol. 10, No. 2, 1987, pp. 103–112.

Premier's Department of New South Wales, *Workforce Planning: A Guide*, Sydney: Premier's Department of New South Wales, 2003.

Reed, Tim, "Determining the Appropriate Size of the Contracting Workforce: Yes We Can!" in *Proceedings of the Eighth Annual Acquisition Research Symposium Thursday Series, Volume II*, 2011.

Schirmer, Peter, *Computer Simulation of General and Flag Officer Management: Model Description and Results*, Santa Monica, Calif.: RAND Corporation, TR-702-OSD, 2009. As of May 16, 2014:
http://www.rand.org/pubs/technical_reports/TR702.html

Schirmer, Peter, Harry Thie, Margaret C. Harrell, and Michael Tseng, *Challenging Time in DOPMA: Flexible and Contemporary Military Officer Management*, Santa Monica, Calif.: RAND Corporation, MG-451-OSD, 2006. As of May 16, 2014:
http://www.rand.org/pubs/monographs/MG451.html

Schwartz, Peter, *The Art of the Long View*, New York: Currency Doubleday, 1996.

Segue Technologies, "USAF 1AM MPES Redevelopment," 2014. As of May 16, 2014:
http://www.seguetech.com/portfolio/usaf-a1m-mpes-redevelopment

Silverman, Joe, Ralph Steuer, and Alan Whisman, "A Multi-Period, Multiple Criteria Optimization System for Manpower Planning," *European Journal of Operational Research*, Vol. 34, No. 2, 1988, pp. 160–170.

Sommers, Dixie, and James C. Franklin, "Employment Outlook: 2010–2020, Overview of Projections to 2020," *Monthly Labor Review*, January 2012.

Sorber, K., and R. Straight, "Measuring Operational Contracting Cost, Output, and Quality Together," in *Proceedings of the Undersecretary of Defense for Acquisition Reform and National Contract Management Association 1995 Acquisition Research Symposium*, Washington, D.C., 1995, pp. 405–418.

Taylor, D. W., P. C. Berry, and C. H. Block, "Does Group Participation When Using Brainstorming Facilitate or Inhibit Creative Thinking?" *Administrative Sciences Quarterly*, Vol. 3, 1958, pp. 23–47.

Trice, Andrew, Kristin Bertelli, and Dan Ward, "Workforce Shaping Models and Metrics in the Public Sector," *People & Strategy*, Vol. 34, No. 3, 2011, pp. 18–27.

Ulrich, Dave, "The Future Targets or Outcomes of HR Work: Individuals, Organizations, and Leadership" in Dan L. Ward, Rob Tripp, and Bill Maki, eds., *Positioned: Strategic Workforce Planning That Gets the Right Person in the Right Job*, New York: AMACOM, 2013.

U.S. Army, Civilian Human Resources Agency, Assistant G-1 for Civilian Personnel, *CIVFORS 101: Part 1: How CIVFORS Generates Forecasts*, 2006.

U.S. Army War College, "How the Army Runs: A Senior Leader Reference Handbook, 2011–2012," 2011.

U.S. Code, Title 10, Armed Forces, Subtitle A—General Military Law, Part I—Organizational and General Military Powers, Chapter 2—Department of Defense, Section 115b, Biennial Strategic Workforce Plan.

U.S. Code, Title 10, Armed Forces, Subtitle A—General Military Law, Part I—Organizational and General Military Powers, Chapter 3—General Powers and Functions, Section 129, Prohibition of Certain Civilian Personnel Management Constraints.

U.S. Department of the Army, "Total Army Analysis (TAA)," Army Regulation 71-11, 1995.

U.S. Department of Defense, DoD Instruction Number 1400.25, Volume 1100, September 9, 2010.

U.S. Department of Health and Human Services, Health Resources and Services Administration, Bureau of Health Professions, *The Physician Workforce: Projections and Research into Current Issues Affecting Supply and Demand*, Washington, D.C.: U.S. Department of Health and Human Services, 2008.

U.S. Department of the Navy, *Career Roadmaps for the Department of the Navy Financial Management (FM) Community*, 2009. As of May 16, 2014: http://www.finance.hq.navy.mil/fmc/PDF/HC-CareerRoadmaps.pdf

U.S. Department of the Navy, *Memorandum for Distribution: Department of Defense (DoD) Financial Management (FM) Civilian Enterprise-Wide Competencies*, 2011.

U.S. Government Accountability Office, *Human Capital: Further Actions Needed to Enhance DoD's Civilian Strategic Workforce Plan*, Washington, D.C.: USGAO, GAO-10-814R, 2010.

U.S. Government Accountability Office, *Defense Acquisitions: Further Action Needed to Better Implement Requirements for Conducting Inventory of Service Contract Activities*, Washington, D.C.: USGAO, GAO-11-192, 2011a.

U.S. Government Accountability Office, *DoD Met Statutory Reporting Requirements on Public-Private Competitions*, Washington, D.C.: USGAO, GAO-11-923R, 2011b.

U.S. Government Accountability Office, *DoD Needs Complete Assessments to Improve Future Civilian Strategic Workforce Plans*, Washington, D.C.: USGAO, GAO-12-1014, 2012a.

U.S. Government Accountability Office, Memo to Congressional Commitees, "Human Capital: Complete Information and More Analyses Needed to Enhance DoD's Civilian Senior Leader Strategic Workforce Plan," Washington, D.C.: USGAO, GAO-12-990R, 2012b.

U.S. Government Accountability Office, *Defense Acquisitions: Continued Management Attention Needed to Enhance Use and Review of DoD's Inventory of Contracted Services*, Washington, D.C.: USGAO, GAO-13-491, 2013.

U.S. Government Accountability Office, *Human Capital: DoD Should Fully Develop Its Civilian Strategic Workforce Plan to Aid Decision Makers*, Washington, D.C.: USGAO, GAO-14-565, 2014.

U.S. Office of Personnel Management, "OPM's Workforce Planning Model," undated. As of August 14, 2014:
http://www.opm.gov/policy-data-oversight/human-capital-management/reference-materials/strategic-alignment/workforceplanning.pdf

U.S. Office of Personnel Management, *Civilian Forecasting System (CIVFORS) 4.0 User's Manual, Version 1.0*, 2003.

Vajda, Steven, *Mathematics of Manpower Planning*, Chichester: Wiley, 1978.

Vernez, Georges, Albert A. Robbert, Hugh G. Massey, and Kevin Driscoll, *Workforce Planning and Development Processes: A Practical Guide*, Santa Monica, Calif.: RAND Corporation, TR-408-AF, 2007. As of May 12, 2014:
http://www.rand.org/pubs/technical_reports/TR408.html

Wang, Jun, *Review of Operations Research Applications in Workforce Planning and Potential Modeling of Military Training*, Land Defense Science and Technology Organisation, Australian Government Department of Defense, DSTO-TR-1688, 2005.

Wang, Jun, *A System Dynamics Simulation Model for a Four-Rank Military Workforce*, Land Defense Science and Technology Organisation, Australian Government Department of Defense, DSTO-TR-2037, 2007.

Ward, D., "Workforce Demand Forecasting Techniques," *Human Resource Planning*, Vol. 19, No. 1, 1996, pp. 54–55.

Ward, Dan L., Rob Tripp, and Bill Maki, eds., *Positioned: Strategic Workforce Planning That Gets the Right Person in the Right Job*, New York: AMACOM, 2013.

Weiner, J. P., "Prepaid Group Practice Staffing and U.S. Physician Supply: Lessons for Workforce Policy," *Health Affairs*, Web exclusive, 2004.